HOSTING THE
KING

An Ancient Strategy for the Kingdom of God in any generation

HOSTING THE
KING

An Ancient Strategy for the Kingdom of God in any generation

INA STEYN

God Is King
over All the Earth

Clap your hands, all peoples!
Shout to God with loud songs of joy!
For the LORD, the Most High,
is to be feared, a great king over all the earth.
He subdued peoples under us, and nations under our feet.
He chose our heritage for us,
the pride of Jacob whom he loves.
Selah.
God has gone up with a shout,
the LORD with the sound of a trumpet.
Sing praises to God, sing praises!
Sing praises to our King, sing praises!
For God is the King of all the earth; sing praises with a psalm!
God reigns over the nations;
God sits on his holy throne.
The princes of the peoples gather as the people of the God of Abraham.
For the shields of the earth belong to God; He is highly exalted!

Psalm 47

Contents

Prologue

You are the salt of the earth;
but if the salt loses its flavour, how shall it be seasoned?
It is then good for nothing but to be thrown out and trampled
underfoot by men.

Matthew 5:13

The Kingdom of God is the essence of the Bible, the culmination of all prophecies, the heartbeat of all history. Much has been written throughout the centuries, and the past decades birthed multiple new views and strategies. There are manifold aspects of this topic, and each book only contributes a little to such a vast topic. The reasons for writing this book are both personal, and yet deeply corporate, rooted in discernment for the times we live in, and the state of our unpreparedness, or rather, our apparent lack of interest in preparing for the Coming Age:

Small Harvest

In the past thirty years I have travelled to many European nations on a regular basis. I have been privileged to meet with people who truly love God, and who are willing to give time and effort to His purposes on earth, even sacrificially. As a public speaker and trainer, I have had the privilege of engaging with groups of leaders and intercessors, and have had many private and personal conversations. Leaders and groups have presented their vision statements and strategies for their ministries. Individuals have shared their dreams and prophetic words to surrender their familiar lives to focus on a particular ministry with the desire to influence our generation for the better, to extend His Kingdom on earth.

The more I listened to passionate, often confused presentations, attending endless leadership meetings, the more I came to realise that a significant component is absent. Figuratively speaking, the flour has been left out of the cake. Many good, quality ingredients are being mixed with great care. The intention is to bake something flavoursome and nutritious. And yet, without flour, the cake cannot rise. It will collapse and fall in on itself once put in any hot oven. It will surely turn out a disaster, a disappointment, not worthy to present to the King.

This discernment was confirmed in follow-up conversations with brave people who continued against the odds for a time in difficult ministries. Often the vision was not clear, or still immature, yet it was launched, resulting in ongoing confusion. Some faced financial difficulties, cultural battles, conflict with those outside the ministry, and conflict with team members and spouses. Some of these faithful ministries continued for years bearing little of the initial anticipated fruit. Many struggled with much uncertainty and pain from the beginning, and never really reached the place where ministry was flourishing, battling the pain of unanswered prayers, much of it interpreted with logical and justifiable reasons.

In too many circumstances, I saw ministries closed down prematurely in a state of inner exhaustion. Prophetic words were put on the shelf as individuals pursued a deeper walk with God, a different approach in another ministry, or simply gave up. Often a different vision was pursued, redefined, relocated and rediscovered, albeit with more trepidation and carefulness; yet, these new attempts did not necessarily bear more fruit. It is as if we lowered the bar, and somehow found a way to be very busy in ministry without reaching the actual goals.

And we accepted this. We just keep going.

My heart breaks for these faithful people, many of them faithful beyond imagination. And my heart mourns the lack of lasting fruit in our generation.

Much Training

As an intercessor in Europe, I am aware that the spiritual realities are quickly shifting in our age. The old battles have now taken on new features and dimensions. Additionally, there are completely new demonic and social aspects opposing us. I have followed the avalanche of daily, bad news alongside all of you.

The fact that confronts me is that we have more missionaries and trained intercessors in this generation than in any generation prior to the twenty-first century. We have more spiritual books, *Youtube* channels, training courses, conferences and webinars available in more languages than ever before. Yet, often the Kingdom of God remains a theological discussion, a prayer burden, and not a reality that is shining forth with glory and justice in our evangelised nations. Rather, the bad news of domestic violence, gender confusion and mental health is daily mocking the Church as the Goliath of old.

What will it take for the Church in the Western world to be victorious in the present acceleration of sin and deterioration, amidst the increased release of confusion, hopelessness and lawlessness? What will make us stop to ask the real questions, and to wait in humility for the reformation necessary to become true apostles as in the first century, who bore much fruit and saw society transformed?

Seeking for Unknown Answers

I wrestled with the above realities, meeting after meeting, week by week, in each mentoring session, and in ongoing prayer. I asked questions of the thinkers, the prophets, and of God. I sensed that we are living on the surface, that we are barely scratching the surface for this generation, and yet, despite the hardship and disappointments, this state of affairs is somehow normalised. My questions were questioned. My wrestling was misunderstood. I now know that I did not even understand my own questions in many stages of this journey.

I became disillusioned with missions, and especially with prophetic and apostolic ministries. I have seen the powerful and the amazing, and yet, these lacked the ability to bear long-lasting fruit. Witnessing the personal and inner confusion of otherwise public, successful Christian leaders made me resistant to living a public ministry that is removed from my inner life. The outward should mirror the inner realities, not cover them up. External ministry should be an overflow from inner abundance, not destroying the inner life for the sake of success on the public platform. I watched. I listened. And I decided that this life of ministry was not for me.

I was leaving Missions after just ten years of joining as an innocent, big-eyed missionary, even although I had been called to fulltime ministry at age eleven. I was confused and amazed at not having seen ministry that was deeply authentic, bearing fruit in nations. I did not trust myself. So, I left it all. I had no plans ahead of me, and had reached the end of seeking and knocking. I was at the end of myself.

In a very gentle conversation with the Lord, He warned me: *Ina, you cannot only be involved in the battle. My calling on your life is to overcome.* I barely coped in my best attempts to merely stay in the game; how could I ever *overcome* in this generation in Europe?

Faithful as God is, when He calls us to new levels, He provides the training to equip and strengthen us to walk it out. This was when I was introduced to a little man wearing a black, monastic habit. My path crossed supernaturally and in an unexpected way with an Orthodox monk, called Father Macarius, of the Orthodox Church of America (OCA).[1] In the next twenty years, Father Macarius introduced and taught me the spiritual principles of the Early Fathers of the Apostolic Age in the first centuries. These men and women lived victoriously with unimaginable spiritual aptitudes, bearing fruit in the nations, even to this day.

As I listened and began to read about these spiritual giants, it became clear to me that the Church has lost much of the original principles and practices of the first Apostolic Church; therefore, we are no longer overcomers in our various cultures and societies. We have become the followers, rather than the trendsetters. The spirit of the world has shaped us to the point that we are not just similar to the world, but actually belong to the world. Our salt has lost its taste.[2] The world permeated us, and now we taste just like the world. The Church has come to have almost no

---

1. **Dr Atef Meshreky** was born in Egypt, and studied medicine, before the Lord called him to be totally set apart as a consecrated celibate brother in the Coptic Church. He later moved to Arizona, USA with his community of monks (*www.stjohnthebaptistaz.org*) and nuns (*www.stmacariusoca.org*). He is tonsured in the OCA (Orthodox Church of America), having received the name **Father Macarius.**
Fifty years ago he started to serve the Lord in full time ministry in upper Egypt. He had an unsatisfied desire for a life of holiness, but when he compared his spiritual reality to the picture of the true Christian life portrayed in the New Testament, he realised a discrepancy. Recurring sins and weaknesses remained inside him, and he deeply yearned for a transformation that would truly bring glory to His Name. After years of prayer and seclusion, the Lord led him to discover the 'wells' of the Early Fathers of the Apostolic Church. These wells, which are forgotten by the Church today, are rich springs and sources of living water of the Church of God that can lead us into deep and fulfilling worship and ministry in the Spirit. Father Macarius has dedicated himself to minister to the body of Christ to deepen spiritual life, enable the Church to face the challenges of the End Times, to reunite the Church of Christ in the East and the West, and to prepare the Bride of Christ for His Second Coming and for the Wedding of the Lamb. His teachings and books are available on *www.shineinternational.org*
2. Matthew 5:13

impact on society, except to be dismissed, even openly rejected and humiliated. In the sixties and seventies, Western society moved beyond respect or fear of God. Today it blatantly laughs at the simple principles of eternity, even directly opposes it. We are called Post-Christian Europe. The Gospel of Jesus Christ – the Good News - no longer shapes society.

Sadly, the Church is so infiltrated with worldly thinking and culture that she does not have the perspective to see how she has been shaped by society. Thus, she battles to remain in the stream of the world, striving not to be left behind, to remain relevant.

Considering the statistics that there are more followers of Christ in more nations in our day than ever before, it is difficult to fathom how the Church has so little influence. If the answer is not in numerical growth and expansion, how should the Church function to bear lasting fruit worthy to present to the King?

I am grieved that most of the present-day Church no longer submits to the Lordship of God. She is increasingly formed by individualists who live and worship according to rational self-will and personal preference, rather than in self-denial and submission to Eternal Truth. I see this as the primary characteristic of the organic church movements who claim to interpret scripture for themselves, in exemption from the wisdom of two thousand years. We 'hear' God for ourselves, and are not accountable to the wisdom gained by those who went before us to align and bridge us with eternity. Our spiritual ears are blocked by humanism and materialism, by political and cultural orientation, and as such, we can barely hear God anymore in His Word.

Luke 8:18: *Take care then how you hear, for to the one who has, more will be given, and from the one who has not, even what he thinks that he has will be taken away.*

Our responsibility and authority as the Church to influence the heavenly realms has been stolen, or have become confused and twisted. Subsequently we blindly labour on earth with limited fruit, or fruit that does not last. We lead young people to the Lord and immediately trumpet the victorious testimonies on social media, to spend five years in counselling and discipleship, only for them to fall back into pornography, drugs and a dark depression without hope.

The heavenly powers sadly dictate the quality of our ministries, instead of us pushing them back in order for His Kingdom to manifest through us in everlasting ways. Multiple ministries spring up all the time. Some flourish. Some struggle. But few open the way for future generations to walk in Revelation and Fear of God. Present-day ministries are restricted to the missionary's presence, while he is still alive. Our fruit no longer extends beyond our lives to open up the way for our descendants to know and serve the Lord and His commandments in even greater ways, to harvest widely in the coming generations.

This book is an endeavour to record my wrestling over the past thirty years. I did not come up with this content in small-group brainstorming, neither is this a product of my own intellect or spiritual abilities. The content of this book was handed down to me, a Western evangelical missionary, by a servant Orthodox monk who spends his life digging the 'wells'[3] of the Early Church Fathers, wells that have been blocked by the evil one through centuries of Church schisms and progressive theological development.

The call to overcome can become a reality if we know and practice eternal principles as revealed in both Testaments,

---

3. Genesis 26:18

and also in the teachings and practices of the Early Church, the records of Church history, and in the prophetic books about the Age to Come when the New Jerusalem will come to reign on a new earth. This is not a book written with fresh insight from our generation, but rather portrays everlasting principles, the divine pattern, set forth for us by a gracious God who longs to save, restore and recreate creation from its fallen state, to bear everlasting fruit.[4]

Our generation is not so unique that the structures, laws and principles which were followed and obeyed for more than six thousand years, both in heaven and on earth, simply 'don't work' for us. This belief underlines not only our stark arrogance and independence, but just how deeply lost we have become. The call is to re-align ourselves with eternity, and to everlasting principles. Then we will see a different quality of fruit in our ministries that will truly glorify God in heaven and on earth.

I am writing this book with spiritual content that Father Macarius has graciously imparted to many over the past five decades. In most of the material, I quote him directly. In other parts, I interpret him (with permission) to make the content understandable to a post-modern reader without an Orthodox or theological background. My intention is not to alter or dilute the spirit of the material, but to make it accessible, akin to the many fragments that were picked up after the multiplication of the bread. If the fullness of the ancient teachings of the Kingdom of God were to be served as a big loaf, we would not know how to bite into it. It would be too foreign, too beyond us in this generation. I trust that these bite-size crumbs will bring Life to each reader, acknowledging that the bigger picture is much more glorious than any single fragment.

---

4.   John 15:16

*Lifting up His eyes, and seeing that a large crowd was coming
toward him, Jesus said to Philip, 'Where are we to buy bread,
so that these people may eat?'*
He said this to test him, for He Himself knew what He would do.
*Philip answered Him, 'Two hundred denarii worth of bread
would not be enough for each of them to get a little.'*
*One of his disciples, Andrew, Simon Peter's brother, said to Him,
'There is a boy here who has five barley loaves and two fish,
but what are they for so many?'*
Jesus said, 'Have the people sit down.'
Now there was much grass in the place.
So the men sat down, about five thousand in number.
*Jesus then took the loaves, and when He had given thanks,
He distributed them to those who were seated.*
So also the fish, as much as they wanted.
*And when they had eaten their fill, He told His disciples,
'Gather up the leftover fragments, that nothing may be lost.'*
*So they gathered them up and filled twelve baskets with
fragments from the five barley loaves left by those who had eaten.*

John 6:5-13

The Kingdom of God

Your kingdom come… on earth as it is in heaven.

Matthew 6:10

The Kingdom of God is the foremost important theme unfolding in history. We find the plans of God to build and establish His Kingdom in each page of the Word of God, from Genesis one until the grand finale in the Book of Revelation. Each Christian should have a deeply-rooted understanding and vision of the Kingdom of God on earth, especially how it will manifest in our generation. Our focus and energy should not be wasted on any other reality but to build and expand the Kingdom of God on earth.

John the Baptist, the forerunner to the Messiah, spent his short public ministry preaching only one message: **Matthew 3:2:** *Repent, for the Kingdom of Heaven is at hand.*

John, the most profound prophet of all times, was teaching and baptising those who came to him in repentance and for forgiveness of sins. We find him at the river Jordan, addressing the empty, religious systems and institutions, preparing the nation of Israel for the King incarnated on earth: *Repent, for the Kingdom of God is at hand!* Any kingdom has a king. The King represents the Kingdom. If the Kingdom of God is near, then the King is near!

This Eternal King of heaven and earth was born thirty years earlier in Bethlehem, Judea. This was a major occasion, and the heavenly hosts sang in jubilation at the joy of His coming. Except for the few bewildered shepherds, it was the outsiders, the gentile kings and magi who came to worship this new-born King:

Matthew 2:1-2: *Now after Jesus was born in Bethlehem of Judea in the days of Herod the king, behold, wise men from the east came to Jerusalem, saying, 'Where is He who has been born King of the Jews? For we saw His star when it rose and have come to worship Him.'*

Once they found Jesus, **Matthew 2:11** reads:
Going into the house they saw the Child with Mary His mother, and they fell down and worshiped Him.

Jesus was born as King on earth. That is absolutely clear from His birth. Jesus' birth on earth brought about an immediate clash between His Kingdom of Light and the dark kingdoms of this world. Therefore, Herod killed all Jewish boys under the age of two, to defend his own kingdom, as Death desires to rule.

Thirty years later, in the fullness of time, John the Baptist proclaimed: *Repent, for the Kingdom of God is at hand.* Through the ministry of John the Baptist, a shift in history manifested. He dedicated the entirety of his short, but powerful ministry to prepare that particular generation for a significant transition: There is a new King on earth! The Eternal Kingdom has come to earth!

His call to repentance was addressed to the Jews, the people of God, a call to prepare, to clear the house, to start over. Repentance implies the Israelites had to turn away from living the way they chose, doing the things they wanted to, to become a people of the new King.

After Jesus' baptism and the forty days of temptation in the wilderness, Jesus started His public ministry with exactly the same message:
Matthew 4:17: *From that time Jesus began to preach, saying, 'Repent, for the kingdom of heaven is at hand.'*

Three years later, Jesus' life on earth came to a brutal climax in His crucifixion, when Pilate nailed unto His cross a placard stating:
John 19:19: *Jesus of Nazareth, the King of the Jews.*

Jesus is Always King

There is no question that Jesus was, and is King. We believe that all Christians belong to His Kingdom. And yet, the concept of the Kingdom of God is still so vague, impractical and distant for many followers of Jesus. There remain many questions that hang like thick fog over our understanding, and these keep us from partaking in our responsibility and eternal calling:

† Has His Kingdom already come, or are we still awaiting His Kingdom?

† What does the Kingdom of God look like in the 21st century?

† Where will we find the Kingdom of God in secular Europe? Or in Islamic Albania?

† What is my role in the Kingdom of God?

† How do we increase His reign on earth? Is it all divinely orchestrated, or is it possible to be involved?

† What is the difference between a conversion experience, and the Kingdom of God?

† What is the difference between the Church, and the Kingdom of God?

† What is the difference between traditional Missions, and the Kingdom of God?

† Will we only see the Kingdom of God in His Second Coming?

† Is it primarily a spiritual reality, a Kingdom in heaven? Or also on earth?

In my short lifespan, I have sat through numerous teachings on this particular topic, and I don't discard any of it. We do have certain dimensions of insight, and I thank God for what the great thinkers have written about this topic in our generation. But there is an ancient component that has not been addressed.

In this book, I will endeavour to introduce a new angle on this topic, acknowledging that I am not a historian, nor an academic theologian, but rather a disciple of this very content. I lack the demand of language about such a magnificent reality, rather, the grandeur of this topic holds me. The content and truth of this little book holds my ministry, my life, and my future. I am found by this content. I lack words to say much, therefore I will use the words of others who are divinely inspired.

I believe that there is a demonic strategy from the ruler of this earth[5] to keep this ancient information from believers, and thus paralyse us in being ineffective in prayer, short-sighted, even barren in ministry. We should live for the increase of His Kingdom, even today.

Many definitions and explanations have been declared around the topic of the Kingdom of God, often biased due to a particular interest or expertise. A business-person, for example, might aim to see increased wealth created and distributed fairly to restore dignity to all strata of society, and also the maximising of gifts in individuals to flourish in the work place. In such a case, the Kingdom of God might be described as a high work-ethic, fair wages, and

---

5.   John 12:31

righteousness and fairness in considering natural gifts, gender and health.

A person focussing on the domain of Family will be highly concerned for divorce rates, adultery, and broken families. They might wrestle with domestic abuse, adoption, and issues related to gender ideology. The Kingdom of God would be defined in a relational way as faithfulness and sacrifice, commitment and love, as forgiveness and belonging. On the other hand, a medical doctor's worldview may express their desire to bring comfort and relief to their patients, to decrease the causes of illnesses. Medical researchers are confronted with the ethics of genetic engineering, the interference with DNA, to create a perfect super-human who is not only strong and intelligent, but also happy and beautiful. The quality of life is debated for or against in the argument of abortion and euthanasia. The question of why God allows pain and suffering is asked. In serving a loving King, is it righteous to decrease pain and suffering at any cost? A social worker dealing with human trafficking may long for justice at the core of the Kingdom of God, whilst a musician or ballerina may argue for the essence of beauty in society.

I listened to many stories. And I wept often with those who struggle and wrestle to see change in society. I honour those who spend their days and lives fighting for righteousness, justice and truth, while not compromising compassion and patience. I thank each one of you who have formed and shaped my life. Because of you I now think wider. I feel deeper. And my prayer life has been radically pruned back, as I can no longer pray fix-it prayers for my generation.

My simple conclusion and desperate quest have always been: There has to be a deeper reality. There has to be a higher way.

And yes, I do believe we left the flour out of this cake recipe. We may fix the flat cake with icing, but it is a disaster. It is not a cake. We should not call it a cake.

The King should be Resident

Any Kingdom without a King is a myth. The bottom-line definition of the Kingdom of God is found in the presence of our Beloved King. Anything besides His presence constitutes the *fruit* of His presence. 'Yes' to a quest for immunisations in poor nations, for fresh water to all, and equal possibilities in education for boys and girls. Yes, we should fight female circumcision in all tribes. Christian parents rightly do not want evolution and gender neutrality to be part of the education of vulnerable youth, and it is necessary that we talk about Climate Change and plastic pollution. However, none of these things would have the impact we long for – to see His Kingdom on earth as it is in heaven - without us starting at the beginning: the Presence of Jesus, the King. This is not a general statement.

We cannot put the cart before the horse. First things first. In Jesus alone is Life. In Jesus alone is redemption and restoration. In Jesus alone do we find the fine balance between justice and compassion, between grace and truth. In Him alone is dignity and hope for the lost. His Kingdom is about His restorative, life-giving presence.

The Presence of Jesus

The concept of the Presence of Jesus is freely and generally interpreted. I would agree that God is graciously present in most of our prayer times and ministries. After all, He is the omnipresent One.[6] However, starting our day with a time of routine prayer does not automatically imply that His presence would confront and overthrow the darkness, and usher in the glory of His Kingdom. Correspondingly, having a Christian ethos during a Board meeting does not routinely manifest His full release in daily ministry.

There must be more!

To see the increase of His presence, even the fullness of His presence, requires us to study the topic of His presence throughout history and eternity. How, and why did God manifest His presence in the past? What are the everlasting practices and protocol, the divine preparations, to see His presence **come**, **increase** and **remain** with a particular people? What are the outcomes once His presence dwells in our midst?

In this book, we will refer to the teachings of the Early Fathers in the first four centuries AD, the first Apostolic Church. I was introduced to the spirituality of the early Fathers, not primarily through content and teaching, but through practice. I had the privilege to 'taste' the presence of Jesus after long liturgical days of prayer and worship. I fellowshipped with men and women who live daily the worship-practices in the spirit of the early Fathers, and their lives have a distinct and different 'flavour.' It confronted me, and made me ask deep questions. I wanted to understand why their spirits were so childlike, so alive, so fresh.

I have only the language of the Word of God, even though I am aware that this language has been interpreted and misinterpreted in each split and schism throughout Church history in various, even extreme ways. But I do

---

6.   Psalm 90:1,2; 139:7-10; Matthew 18:20; 28:20

pray that these seemingly familiar concepts will be dusted and polished to shine with the initial freshness of the first centuries.

How?

God never acts in response to Satan. He always leads, and never follows. He is sovereignly in control at all times. History is in His hands, and He is unfolding the future in a definite way.

Isaiah 46:9-10: *For I am God, and there is no other; I am God, and there is none like Me, declaring the end from the beginning and from ancient times things not yet done, saying, 'My counsel shall stand, and I will accomplish all my purpose.'*

God has been faithful through the ages to lead each generation forward towards His ultimate purposes on earth, according to His timing and seasons, for the complete manifestation of His Kingdom on earth. So how does God build His Kingdom on earth?

This is an immense question, which we will unfold in coming chapters. God cannot be manipulated, or commanded, to come and dwell on earth. He is holy. In order to really influence the spiritual atmosphere in our generation and nations, we need to adhere to His holy, eternal ways to experience His actual presence on earth. We should yield our understanding and distinctive generational convictions to His if we long to see His Kingdom extending into future generations.

We should discover the eternal principles and ways of the King and His Kingdom in the different stages since creation. We will find that He has always called His people to establish peculiar places of worship, strongholds to hold His throne on earth, a dwelling place from where He can reach out to the nations with authority, to heal and to restore.

In coming chapters, we will be journeying together throughout history.

Divine Union on Earth

The LORD God caused a deep sleep to fall upon the man,
and while he slept took one of his ribs and closed up its place with flesh.
And the rib that the LORD God had taken from the man
He made into a woman
and brought her to the man. Then the man said,
'This at last is bone of my bones and flesh of my flesh;
she shall be called Woman, because she was taken out of Man.'

Genesis 2:21-23

God is King, and He wants to rule on earth. This is the only way for the earth and all its inhabitants to flourish, prosper and reach its fullness. There is no life outside of His Kingdom. His rulership is our only hope of happiness, peace and everlasting life.

Ever since the Fall, God set His heart on restoring all of creation, both heaven and earth, in His Kingdom rule. God has no aspirations to rule from afar, from the distant heavens. Since the beginning of creation, it has always been His desire to rule from within our midst. God wants to be with us, and near us. He wants to fill our lives with His peace, glory, and life-giving breath. He does not only want to give us gifts, provide angelic protection, or answer prayers - these being precious blessings. Rather, God is covenantal and longs to dwell, even within us, not only in our midst.

We were created in the image of a Trinitarian Relationship for one purpose: for God to unite Himself with mankind, so that His Kingdom can be established on earth through mankind.

The first two chapters in the book of Genesis give us an account of the beginning of creation. The question is often posed how creation might have unfolded in future chapters had the Fall never occurred? Would the book of Genesis have continued to give more details of God's act of creating, or were all the necessary facts already established and revealed in the first two chapters?

I believe many more books could have been written detailing God's objectives and intentions for creation. God would have shared with us His heart about His Kingdom on earth, His plans for mankind to discover His heart, until its fullness was able to materialise in perfection on earth through mankind. I believe God would have introduced mankind to His eternal purposes, trained us, and sealed this with His loving holiness. The first two chapters of Genesis were only the beginning of creation, not the finished version.

It was as though the Fall halted the pen of the writer, as if God's conversation with mankind was temporarily interrupted in order to first solve the problem of sin. Only then would God be able to resume the conversation with mankind about His everlasting mysteries and heart's desires.

Unity in Eden

In the beginning, God created man, granted him everything, and started a dialogue with him. As the Eternal Father, from day one, God led Adam and taught him in a fatherly manner about wisdom, discernment and the ways of obedience leading to everlasting life. He was jealously watching over Adam. He began to explain to Adam what he could and could not eat. Every detail was of great importance to God. These 'teaching sessions' did not happen from afar in a show of authority and legalities, but rather in an intimate setting of trust, worship and wonder.

Genesis 2:16-17: *The LORD God commanded the man, saying, 'You may surely eat of every tree of the garden, but of the tree of the knowledge of good and evil you shall not eat, for in the day that you eat of it you shall surely die.'*

This was not a restrictive conversation, but a conversation to hold and protect Adam, to ensure a future for him.

God also introduced Adam to creation, as mankind was to rule and have dominion over all.

Genesis 1:28: *God blessed them. And God said to them, 'Be fruitful and multiply and fill the earth and subdue it, and have dominion over the fish of the sea and over the birds of the heavens and over every living thing that moves on the earth.'*

It is unknown how long these exchanges lasted, but there was much to discover in the Garden, and God was mentoring Adam in reigning over all of the earth. We can imagine a father-son relationship of walking through the garden, discovering, explaining, whilst wonder and love filled Adam's heart. God was introducing creation to Adam in mutual togetherness. He was preparing Adam to rule on earth. This relationship of love between God and man, between Master and student, between Creator and created, between Father and son of God[7] set the tone for the future. God was not only visiting the Garden at certain times in the day. No. He was dwelling on earth with Adam. Adam was filled with the fullness of God as God breathed into him the Breath of Life, which is all of Himself, the everlasting Life-giver.

Genesis 2:7: *Then the LORD God formed the man of dust from the ground and breathed into his nostrils the breath of life, and the man became a living creature.*

After naming the animals, the next stage in creation began to unfold, the mystery of marital union. At this stage, God had already taught Adam what, and what not to eat; and how to rule over the animals. Adam had grown in his insight of God's principles on earth, and was ready to participate in the next stage of the unfolding of the Kingdom of God on earth.

---

7.   Luke 3:38

It was time to create a helpmate for Adam. Adam had matured enough for God to teach him about love, marriage and union. This was a significant and delicate stage as the eternal mystery of the Marriage of the Son of God with mankind was beginning to be revealed on earth. The second Person of the Trinity longed to be united with mankind, not in a general way, but in a Bridal way. This Bridal union would seal the Kingdom of God on earth, forever and ever.

Therefore, it was time for Eve to be created, and to be presented to Adam.

Genesis 2:22-24: *The rib that the LORD God had taken from the man He made into a woman and brought her to the man. Then the man said, 'This at last is bone of my bones and flesh of my flesh; she shall be called Woman, because she was taken out of Man.' Therefore a man shall leave his father and his mother and hold fast to his wife, and they shall become one flesh.*

God started to disclose to Adam the mystery of marriage, the bridal mystery, the mystery of Christ and His bride. You may wonder how the mystery of Christ and the Church was a reality before the Fall? In **Ephesians chapter 5**, apostle Paul speaks about this eternal bridal mystery when he quotes **Genesis chapter 2**. Since before the Fall, in all eternity, God had purposed Bridal unity between mankind and the Word who spoke creation into being, Jesus the second Person of the Trinity. God created us through the Son, who is the Bridegroom. We were created for Him, and in His image.

This is partly why God did not create for Adam a mate in the beginning, as He did for all the other living creatures. It was not a mistake, as if God accidently overlooked creating a mate for Adam. God did not suddenly realise that Adam was lonely, and then reconfigured His plan. It was all part of the unfolding of the mystery that each bridegroom has a bride. Adam also has a bride. The Word of God has a Bride. Right from the beginning, God was allowing mankind to partake in His longing for a partner to love, to share in the longing of God's own heart.

Therefore, it was necessary for Adam to have waited for Eve. The longing in Adam's heart for a soulmate was but an echo of the desire in God's heart to love with all of His Being another that is different from Him, and yet similar to Him.

Thus, God created the woman from Adam, and presented her to Adam to be given a name. Adam called her Eve.[8] He recognised her as his flesh, bone of his bones. And yet, union between Adam and Eve would be a process. They had to discover their similarities, and their differences. They were growing to become one unit. Was this unity on the level of the flesh only?

No. God is Spirit. Mankind was created in God's image for everlasting spiritual union. God was beginning to reveal a spiritual unity that was deeply mystical, pure and everlasting. This union was to be between finite humans and an infinite God. It was a union between the created and the Creator. This union would manifest His Kingdom on earth, a Kingdom of covenantal love.

Isaiah 54:5: *For your Maker is your husband, the LORD of hosts is His Name.*

This unexpected, unlikely union would manifest His Kingdom on earth for all birds, fish and mankind to live in peace and worship to their Creator. Each creature would find their distinct place without comparison or competition,

---

8. Genesis 3:20

without fear.[9] It would be more than a co-existence, or 'unity in diversity.' It could never be a passive Kingdom where the negative is simply absent. The Kingdom of God would be alive, pulsating with Godly-life, brightness and beauty from within creation. The Kingdom would be evolving and eternally revealing the depths of His infinite and omnipotent nature of holiness and love, and glorify Him as a King in all His magnificence.

Created in the Image of the Son

The Son is the Person of the Trinity to reveal to mankind the fullness of God Eternal. It is God's intention that mankind is to be united with the Son, to come to the full knowledge of the infinite God and His Kingdom on earth.

John 1:18: *No one has seen God at any time; the Only-begotten Son, who is in the bosom of the Father, He has declared Him.*

God granted to all of creation a very clear image and picture of God for all to realise and understand its unseen Creator. Who is the Image of God? The Son is the Image, since before the foundation of the earth.[10] Mankind was created in this Image.

In the incarnation of Jesus, the second Person of the Trinity, the Word of God, would take upon Him our humanity to restore the original Image in which we were created, the Image of Jesus Himself, which was marred in the fall.

Colossians 1:15: *He [Jesus] is the image of the invisible God, the First-born of all creation.*

---

9.   Isaiah 11:6-8; 65:25
10.   John 1:14; Ephesians 1:4

Hebrews 1:3: *Who, being…the express image of His essence, and upholding all things by the word of His power, through Himself cleansing of our sins, He sat down on the right of the Majesty on high.*

Today we have a poor understanding of what 'to be created in God's image' implies. It is often reduced to the concept that God is the origin, and we are the mirror-image. However, the Son, being the Image of God, is not only a reflection or shadow of the authentic, original version. Jesus is God Himself, consubstantial with the Father.

Mankind was created in the Image of the Son, the spoken Word, because mankind was from the beginning intended to unite with God in Bridal union. That is why the Word became flesh and dwelt on earth for our salvation, restoration and realisation of eternal purposes on earth.

John 1:14: *The Word became flesh and dwelt among us, and we have seen His glory, glory as of the only Son from the Father, full of grace and truth.*

The Fall interrupted the unfolding of events. Yet, God's eternal purposes were not side-lined. God is our Husband and Redeemer;[11] **He will reign eternally on earth through bridal union with mankind.**

The state of man in Paradise before the Fall is impossible for us to imagine. The distortion and darkening of our minds in the Fall make it inconceivable to comprehend such perfection, how pure union with God was possible. We have to re-learn these mysteries of union with the Bridegroom, once His redemption renews and restores us. Through the sacrifice of the Body and Blood of Jesus

---

11. Isaiah 54:5

Christ our Saviour, and especially in His resurrection and ascension, we can again attain to union with God, to partake in His divine nature.[12]

†

But let us go back to the Garden of Eden, and the initial relationship between God and Adam. We said they named all the creatures, which was followed by the creation of Eve. Adam was used to hearing the voice of God in the Garden. They would walk in the cool of the day, conversing lovingly and joyfully as members of one family.

Genesis 3:8ᵃ (LITV): *They heard the sound of the LORD God walking up and down in the garden at the breeze of the day.*
Genesis 3:8ᵃ (ESV): *They heard the sound of the LORD God walking in the garden in the cool of the day.*

The 'breeze of the day', also translated as 'the windy time of the day,' was tenderly filled with creativity and revelation through the Holy Spirit. The 'breeze' refers to the breath of God, the Spirit of God; the life-giving grace on earth. These times were true fellowship in all-encompassing peace, birthing new things from God's heart on earth. This was creation in action, unfolding delicately and carefully, like an actual birth taking place.

This perfect life-giving relationship between God and mankind would have continued and matured according to His divine plan. God was on the verge of revealing to Adam about marital unity in body, soul and spirit.

Genesis chapter 2 ends as the topic of marriage starting to be revealed. As God began to introduce this new

---

12.   2Peter 1:4

stage between Himself and mankind, Satan frantically interjected. **Genesis chapter 3** opens with the statement of the serpent, the enemy. This led to deception, confusion, and disobedience. The poison of the serpent abruptly interrupted the discovery and unfolding of the Bridal mystery.

The enemy sensed that Adam was soon to enter into the full understanding of the eternal matters that would seal the Kingdom of God on earth. In his envy, the enemy wanted to break the chain at this crucial point, to halt the possibility of complete union of mankind with God. The enemy could not tolerate being an outcast forever, denied any rulership. He knew that perfect union between mankind and God would be the end of his own aspirations to rule on earth. As such, he manifested at this delicate time with deceit.

The conversations that were destined to take place between God and His creation were temporarily halted. Without maturity and purity, mankind could not grasp the desire of God's heart to rule on earth in Bridal union. Once the destruction of the Fall took place, God distributed the mysteries that Adam should have received throughout future generations. God would reveal His purposes, His ways and His heart to mankind, one step at a time, because God's plans could never be deviated or cancelled.

It is impossible for God to unite with fallen mankind; thus, the consequences of the Fall, as recorded in **Genesis chapter 3,** were that Adam and Eve were cast out from the Garden of Fellowship, separated from the Divine Presence.[13] And yet, as God's mind and heart is unchanging, He prophetically proclaimed the redemption of mankind[14] to bring about His Kingdom purposes.

---

13. Genesis 2:17
14. Genesis 3:15

This same destructive impact of sin on mankind manifested in the lives of Cain and his descendants,[15] until the degrading level of devastation we read about in **Genesis chapter 6**, when God regretted that He had ever created man on earth.[16] Mankind did not value God's intentions, and the following chapters of Genesis expose the depth of corruption within mankind and all of creation. We continue to read about Nimrod, and the tower of Babel.[17] These were devastating times.

Thank God, in **Genesis chapter eleven** we find an individual called Abram responding to God, and from him was formed a nation called Israel. This was a definite new beginning in history. Throughout the coming generations, God's love and eternal purposes continued to be revealed, both holy and uncompromisingly, yet always gracious and compassionate. God taught, guided and shepherded with clear instructions, patience and grace. Throughout this careful, slow process of revealing Himself and His character, He laid a foundation that would last for generations, highlighting a superior plan, greater than only the salvation of individuals from sin and eternal condemnation.

The Kingdom plan on earth was unfolding. God wants to dwell with mankind as King. God wants to be united with mankind. God wants to rule through mankind on earth.

He is the King, and His Kingdom will bring righteousness and peace on earth.

---

15.   Genesis 4
16.   Genesis 6:5-6
17.   Genesis 10-11

A Dwelling Place for God

Let them make Me a sanctuary, that I may dwell in their midst.

Exodus 25:8

The following principles are eternal, rather than mere strategic possibilities for short-term results. God intentionally revealed His heart's objectives to mankind through the centuries. These principles are the ways of God in the past, and for the future. These can be identified as far back as the book of Genesis, and they continue to unfold in their exact format throughout the generations. We see the same principles in the New Testament with the birth of the Church. There are no other principles for us to submit to and pursue as we enter into the End Times, if we long to see His Kingdom on earth in our generation.

This does not leave us with the freedom to pick or choose our options and preferences. These are God's everlasting ways, and they remain to be the only road map for us, even in the 21st century.

God implemented these principles in laying the foundation for a tabernacle in the midst of Israel, a place of dwelling for the Holy One. Later in history, the tabernacle was replaced by the building of a permanent temple in Jerusalem. And eventually, in the fullness of time Jesus, the Son of God, came to *dwell* in a human body on earth.[18]

Foundational Components

† A Leader
† A Tent
† An Altar (with sacrifices)
† Priesthood

---

18.   John 1:14

In history we take notice that each time, when all these above-mentioned components were in place, God would come in full dimensions of His presence to dwell with His people. His presence was accompanied with documented lists of blessings (health, rain, harvest, multiplication and increase, victory and peace).[19] His Kingdom manifested on earth, if the King had a place to dwell.

The word *dwell* is central to the revelation of His Kingdom in our midst. The root meaning of the word is 'to tent,' or 'to camp.' A tent is a temporary living space which is able to move with the changing of seasons and demands of life. Surrounding nations always acknowledged the superiority of the God of Israel over their own gods because, unlike them, He dwelt amongst His people with loving care. Thus, the nations feared the God of Israel.

The above principles will be individually discussed in following chapters.

How can we not follow His eternal principles to establish a place for the King in our midst? How can we not pursue His dwelling presence in our midst as our first priority? This is the only way for the Great I Am, with His river of Life, to flow into our nations and bring healing to racial conflict, unjust poverty, bitterness, depression and hopelessness. This is the only way to secure a future for coming generations.

Ministries built without these eternal principles may bear fruit for a season, but lack the ability to unlock eternal realities for coming generations. These ministries are often only seasonal, and sadly they primarily bear the characteristics of the pioneering apostle, rather than the imprint of an Eternal King. They are evangelistic groups,

---

19.   Deuteronomy 28

prophetic schools, or teaching courses, but are limited and time-bound both in ministry, and in its fruit.

We should rather build to endure into all eternity.

We will look at how these principles were revealed and manifested in different phases on earth.

Overview from the Old Testament

In each stage of history, God followed the same eternal plan. He consistently communicated His divine plan to a chosen leader. No dwelling place for God can ever be built through mere personal inspiration, nor through individualistic creativity and generational thinking. God calls, sets apart and anoints these chosen ones to establish deep foundations to host His presence, to build His throne, to bear fruit in coming generations.

Following the Fall, the Spirit began to teach the family of **Adam** about preparing a place where He could meet with them outside the gates of the Garden of Eden. God taught them the necessity of a blood sacrifice made upon an altar in a posture of worship and humility. In **Genesis chapter 4**, it becomes apparent that the expected blessings and presence of God cannot manifest by any arbitrary offering. In this chapter, the motives of the heart are exposed, and the righteous and unrighteous are identified and segregated. While God is compassionate and gracious, He is uncompromising in His eternal ways.

After the Flood, we see another new beginning in **Genesis 8:20**. As **Noah** left the ark, everything in the world being washed away, the first thing he did was to build an altar unto the Lord. He took from every clean animal and bird, and offered a burnt offering on this altar. This altar refers to the restoration of fellowship between God and mankind after the Flood. God was once again teaching mankind to understand how to fellowship with a holy God, and to draw Him near. This altar dedicated the earth anew to the Lord. As the priestly offering was accepted in heaven, God's Lordship was again declared on earth.

Similarly, **Abraham** responded to God's call in building altars to the Lord.

Genesis 12:7-8: *The LORD appeared to Abram and said, 'I will give this land to your seed.' And he built an altar there to the LORD who appeared to him. And he moved from there to a mountain on the east of Bethel. And he pitched his tent with Bethel toward the sea and Hai on the east. And he built an altar there to the LORD, and called upon the Name of the LORD.*

As Abraham sojourned in obedience to God, he continuously and faithfully pitched his tent and built an altar to the Lord.[20] He called on the Name of the Lord – a testimony of continuous fellowship with God. Abraham was journeying through a land promised to his descendants, and he would intentionally dedicate the land to his God by offering to Him acceptable sacrifices on an altar. God responded to Abraham's offering, and He sealed the land with His authority. No longer could the pagan gods rule in their destructive ways on the land allotted to God's people. The physical Promised Land - the soil, rivers, plants and animals - were consecrated to God as He abided on the altars of Abraham. His Kingdom manifested through Abraham in Israel.

---

20. Genesis 12:1-7; 12:8-13; 13:14-18; 22:9-14

The material creation groans in the absence of the dwelling of its Creator King.[21] Nature can only be restored if the King rules on an altar, an earthly throne.

Abraham's altars were always connected with his tent, which was more than just his temporary, mobile accommodation in this foreign land where he owned no land. He always prioritised the altar of God wherever he moved. Consequently, his own personal tent became the tent of God, the place from which God's grace flowed, and His authority was manifested; a meeting place with heaven. Abraham's tent became a dwelling place, a sanctuary for God.

The tent is a reminder to us that we do not belong anywhere permanently. We should always have our hearts free from the earth, lifted up in obedience to a superior vision. Our real citizenship is in heaven. While on earth, we only live in tents, and our tents should have an altar kindled with a burning sacrifice to our King.

Moses and Israel

God sent His chosen people, the descendants of Abraham, to Egypt, until the sins of the gentile nations living in the Promised Land were completely filled up, and they could be righteously judged.[22]

In the Book of Exodus, after four hundred and thirty years, God brought Israel out of Egypt and led them through the desert towards their Promised Land. Once they crossed the Red Sea, God called Moses and seventy elders up the

---

21.   Romans 8:22
22.   Genesis 15:16

burning mountain of God[23] and shared with them His heart. He gave them exact instructions on how to build a tabernacle, a sanctuary, so that He could descend from the mountain and dwell in their camp, in their midst. He does not like the distance between Himself and mankind.

Exodus 25:8: *Let them make Me a sanctuary, so that I may dwell among them.*

Israel was no longer an individual, nor a family, but had become a nation. It becomes apparent that the principles were especially established for the corporate, and would not change in future generations.

The instructions given to Moses on the burning mountain are summarized in **Exodus chapters 25 and 26.** We read that Moses did everything according to what the Lord commanded him earlier; he built a tent, he established an altar, and he sanctified a priesthood.[24] Once every detail was completed in exact obedience to God, we can expect everlasting results:

Exodus 40:34,35: *The cloud covered the tabernacle of the congregation* [Tent of Meeting], *and the glory of the LORD filled the tabernacle. Moses was not able to enter into the tabernacle of the congregation because the cloud stayed on it, and the glory of the LORD filled the tabernacle.*

God's presence dwelt in the midst of His chosen people, and the Israelites experienced the fullness of the Lord's blessings and power for them.

---

23. Exodus 24

24. **Exodus 40:16:** *Moses did so. According to all that the LORD commanded him, so he did.*

Moses was a forerunner of the Messiah. He built a particular tent for God. He established a certain altar for God, and took care that the fire on the altar never went out. Consequently, God's presence rested in the midst of Israel, and He personally led them carefully, like a mother would lead her young, through the desert.[25] The glory of God shone amidst the nations. It was most fearful and majestic. An ancient Jewish proverb goes: *God is not a nice uncle. God is an earthquake.* Indeed!

This was only the beginning of God revealing His eternal intentions. The fullness of His desire was expressed in His first conversation with Moses on Mount Sinai:

Exodus 19:5-6: *Now, if you will obey My voice indeed, and keep My covenant, then you shall be a peculiar treasure to Me above all the nations; for all the earth is Mine. You shall be to Me a kingdom of priests and a holy nation. These are the words which you shall speak to the sons of Israel.*

This revelation is foundational to anything we can ever imagine or understand about the Kingdom of God on earth, and defines the heart of this book.

Joshua walked closely with Moses, and knew how to stand in the holy Presence of the Lord.[26]

Exodus 33:11[b]: *When Moses turned again into the camp, his assistant Joshua the son of Nun, a young man, would not depart from the tent.*

Joshua knew that the divine Presence carries the Authority of the heavenly Kingdom. The greatest treasure, the only

---

25. Deuteronomy 1:31
26. Exodus 24

weapon Israel had, was the glorious, burning Presence in their midst. Obedience and worship were their primary calling and identity as a nation. Fighting battles was not priority. Without this inner clarity and focus Joshua could not have lead Israel into victory.

Joshua served God till the end of his life,[27] and won many battles,[28] but his victories cannot be separated from his faithful worship in the tent of God, at the altar of God. He had a priestly heart, and walked in supernatural authority among the nations, losing no battles, unless there was sin in the camp.[29]

Joshua 24:15: *But as for me and my house, we will serve the LORD.*

David was both a worshipper and king, and was victorious in all his battles. It is unto David that God imprinted the detailed blueprint for the building of a permanent temple, because of his sensitive heart and absolutely obedience to God.

It is significant that these plans were not directly given to Solomon, who would built the temple.[30] Although Solomon was considered to be the wisest man on earth, David was the man who was found worthy to be entrusted with God's heart's intentions, the earthly expression of His eternal ways – to build a dwelling place for the King to rule in the midst of Israel.

1Chronicles 28:19: *All this He made clear to me in writing from the hand of the LORD, all the work to be done according to the plan.*

---

27. Joshua 24:31
28. Joshua 12:7 onwards
29. Joshua 7
30. 1Chronicles 22:8-10

David knew God's heart[31] and the principles of His Kingdom. He enabled his descendants to experience the peace and prosperity of the Kingdom of God on earth in their midst.

The New Testament

In the fullness of time,[32] Jesus was incarnated.

John 1:14[a]: *The Word became flesh and dwelt among us.*

According to the original language, the phrase 'dwelt among us' means to 'built His tent among us.' In other English translations, this phrase reads 'tented among us' (Apostolic Bible Polyglot), 'tabernacled among us' (Literal translation), and 'did tabernacle among us' (Young literal translation).

God descended to live in a tent on earth, within a human body. The fullness of His glory was once again dwelling in a temporary tent, just as in **Exodus chapter 40**, or in **1Kings chapter 8**, when His presence filled Moses' tabernacle and Solomon's temple.

Our temporary bodies are a type of tent, and in due time we will lift our tent pegs to go to our eternal home. Both apostles Paul and Peter referred to their own departure in these terms. Peter writes in his last epistle in **2Peter 1:14**: *Knowing that shortly I must put off my tent...*

Apostle Paul also describes his departure as a time 'to dismantle his tent' if we compare different translations of **2Timothy 4:6**: *For I am already being poured out as a drink offering, and the time of my departure is at hand.* (KJV)

---

31.   Acts 13:22[b]
32.   Galatians 4:4

In Jesus we see again the fullness of God's glory dwelling on earth.

Colossians 2:9: *For in Him the whole fullness of deity dwells bodily.*

The human body of Christ became the temporary tabernacle in which the Presence of God dwelt.[33] Jesus is the dwelling place of the fullness of God on earth.

Jesus fulfilled all the requirements mentioned earlier. He was the High priest, not according to Levitical standards, but in the order or Melchizedek. Jesus was in constant prayer to His Father, whilst surrendering His own will in sacrificial obedience at all times. His body, and each day of His earthly life, was a sacrifice. In the fullness of time, the Cross became His altar.

Jesus crossed into a new dispensation in time. On Resurrection Sunday, once He conquered sin and death, He breathed on the disciples His Spirit.[34] No longer would the Spirit of God only dwell in Christ, but now dwelt in His apostles. Their physical bodies have become tents on earth for the glory of God to dwell within, for His Kingdom to extent its rule on earth.[35] This *new tent* of the Church, His spiritual body, manifested after Pentecost.

In the epistle to the Hebrews the author explains to us the parallelisms and similarities we find in both Testaments:

† Our body is a **tent** in which He longs to increasingly

---

33. Colossians 1:15
34. John 20:22
35. **Ephesians 5:30:** *Members of His body, of His flesh and of His bones.*

dwell.[36] We are only in temporary accommodation. We do not belong to the earth, and we do not hold anything dear which we cannot take with us into eternity. This is a call to be set apart from the world, to be set apart to God to hold His presence, pleasing God always;[37] a call to absolute obedience to God.[38]

✝ Jesus is the eternal **altar** of our lives. Our lives should be united with the Crucified One, to die daily to ourselves. We carry the Cross of Jesus within our hearts, in our lives.

✝ Any altar demands a sacrifice. God does not respond to an empty and neglected altar. His presence only comes on altars where our daily sacrifices continually burn. We are to present all of our lives as a sacrifice unto God.[39] Our sacrifices are renewed daily as we fellowship with the Holy One.[40] We lose our lives for Him, to find our lives in Him.
Colossians 3:3[b]: *...and your life is hidden with Christ in God.*

✝ In Christ, I become the **priest** of my own, inner altar in a vertical stance at my inner altar, as I bring my daily offerings and incense to God.[41] I minister to God first of all in my heart. I also bless others in His Name, and minister to others in love and compassion.

We will look at our priestly role in chapter 12.

---

36. 1Corinthians 3:16,17
37. Galatians 1:10
38. Philippians 2:5-11
39. Romans 8:36; 12:1-3
40. Galatians 6:14; 1Corinthians 1:18, 2:2; Philippians 1:29, 3:10; Hebrews 13:13
41. Romans 12:1-2, Hebrews 13:15,16

The End Times

The **Apostle John** on the island of Patmos was entrusted with the revelation of the mystery of the Holy City coming down from heaven: the final dwelling of God with man on earth in the New Jerusalem. The eternal principles once again clearly manifest: there is a 'tent', but this time it is an eternal, newly built city, called Zion. There is an altar where the blood of the Lamb will speak of grace and forgiveness forever.[42] Finally, there is a priesthood, comprised of the High priest Jesus Christ, and the redeemed who are gathered at the heavenly altar.

The fullness of His presence will be brighter than the sun,[43] and His Kingdom will extend to all the earth, and to all nations.

†

In each of these individual biblical stages and leaders mentioned above, we recognise the eternal principles of establishing a Dwelling Place for God in the midst of His people, manifesting His Kingdom on earth in their generation:
1. God chose a person, and this godly person received clear instructions in his heart about 2. a tent, 3. an altar with sacrifices, and 4. about a priesthood.

If these principles are exactly adhered to in humility and awe in any generation, the presence of the mighty God will come and dwell in our midst, and establish His reign in our lives.

---

42. Revelation 8:3,5
43. Revelation 22:5

His presence increased and intensified in each dispensation throughout history, from the humble, hidden presence on Abraham's altar to the glorious presence of God within Jesus on the Mount of Transfiguration, until the Grand Finale manifesting the complete restoration in the Second Coming of Christ, when He will rule and reign, united with the Bride, on the new earth. And His Kingdom shall last forever.

I saw the Holy City, New Jerusalem,
coming down out of heaven from God,
prepared as a Bride adorned for her Husband.
And I heard a loud voice from the throne saying,
'Behold, the dwelling place of God is with man.
He will dwell with them, and they will be His people,
and God Himself will be with them as their God.'

Revelation 21:2,3

Spiritual Dwelling Places

How lovely is your dwelling place, O LORD of hosts!
My soul longs, yes, faints for the courts of the LORD;
my heart and flesh sing for joy to the living God.
Even the sparrow finds a home, and the swallow a nest for herself,
where she may lay her young,
at your altars, O LORD of hosts, my King and my God.
Blessed are those who dwell in your house, ever singing your praise!
Selah
Blessed are those whose strength is in You,
in whose heart are the highways to Zion.
As they go through the Valley of Baca they make it a place of springs;
the early rain also covers it with pools.
They go from strength to strength; each one appears before God in Zion.
O LORD God of hosts, hear my prayer; give ear, O God of Jacob!
Selah
Behold our shield, O God; look on the face of your anointed!
For a day in your courts is better than a thousand elsewhere.
I would rather be a doorkeeper in the house of my God
than dwell in the tents of wickedness.
For the LORD God is a sun and shield;
the LORD bestows favour and honour.
No good thing does he withhold from those who walk uprightly.
O LORD of hosts, blessed is the one who trusts in you!

Psalm 84

Building an altar for the Lord, a dwelling place for God, is language frequently used, especially in Prayer and Intercessory ministries in our generation. I find that there is much confusion, even misuse of this language. The strategy on how to build such an altar usually differs from group to group, which does not make sense when viewed in eternity. God is eternal, and His ways are the same throughout the ages. He does not change. How is it possible that there are such a variety of interpretations on how to host His presence, or how to establish a dwelling place for Him, who is the same yesterday, today and forever?

Certain everlasting building blocks are necessary to make an eternal impact on any generation. Building in these eternal ways will not only bring about His full blessing and favour in any particular generation, but it will unlock the Gospel for future generations to know Him, love Him, obey His truth in healthy fear.

Since the early 90s, movements of prayer have spread across the nations in unprecedented ways. Praise God for this gracious movement through His Holy Spirit. From Brazil to the Philippines, from Korea and throughout Africa, the Holy Spirit led intercessors and church leaders to build Houses of Prayer, Tabernacles of Prayer, Prayer Mountains, Prayer rooms, Pillars of Prayer, War rooms, Forerunner ministries, Boiler rooms, 24/7 prayer rooms - just to mention a few.

Similar scripture verses are often used by these groups of eager worshippers:

Isaiah 62:6: *I have set watchmen on your walls, O Jerusalem, who will not always be silent all the day nor all the night; you who remember the LORD, do not be silent.*

Ezekiel 22:30: *I sought for a man among them, that should make up the hedge, and stand in the gap before me for the land, that I should not destroy it: but I found none.*

Leviticus 6:13: *The fire shall always be burning on the altar. It shall never go out.*

Luke 2:36-37: *There was a prophetess, Anna… She was advanced in many days, and had lived with a husband seven years from her virginity. She was a widow of eighty-four years, who did not depart from the temple, serving God with fastings and prayers night and day.*

Mark 11:17: *Is it not written, 'My house shall be called the house of prayer for all nations?'*

I would often come across **Jeremiah 6:16:** *So says the Lord, stand in the ways and see, and ask for the ancient paths where the good way is, and walk in it, and you shall find rest for your souls.*

It is, without any doubt, clear that the Holy Spirit is speaking to us about an important cry in His own heart:
I do not simply want to manifest in your meetings. Build a dwelling place for Me.

I am convinced that all these diverse prayer ministries were birthed through the preparatory work of the Holy Spirit for a time like this, despite the methods varying significantly in different expressions, denominations and cultures. Usually, much time is spent in worship (in our Western understanding of worship), and in intercession (by definition, intercession is prayer for others as led by the Holy Spirit). In many ministries, room is made for children and youth to join with older generations to come before God in bringing the issues at hand before Him in prayer. Creativity plays a central place, with crayons and art material, musical instruments and flags. Gradually, issues of Social Justice surfaced prominently in the strategies and agenda. Messianic symbolism and feasts were often an added component, if not central.

God was not necessarily the focus in Prayer. Sadly, particular and specific burdens became the focus and goal of such Houses of Prayer: the Injustice and Corruption of Human Trafficking, Zion and the restoration of Israel, Islam and Unreached People Groups etc. Many prayer groups focused on revival for their city, or nation. Prayer material would be researched, shared and presented before the Lord in the scheduled prayer times throughout the day and / or week. The focus was the felt-need, sin and the lost, trauma and chaos, or the latest political upheaval in the news. And there was always the unfailing presence of a coffee-corner.

I write with great sadness that God was not always the clear and obvious centre of it all, even although the intentions of the founders were initially burning with clarity. Although God is the Saviour, the means to the answers to our prayers, whom we petition to respond to our cries, the real focus often was the crisis, unrighteousness, the darkness in society.

Over time, many of these ministries added silence as a key component to their daily activities, an introduction to contemplation or *Lectio Divina* – an ancient way of ruminating the Word of God in prayer.

As I travelled and listened to those faithfully standing in the gap for their communities, I came to realize that the same terminology and scripture passages were frequently used, although rarely with deep, biblical understanding. Each person and ministry had taken the responsibility to interpret the calling of the Holy Spirit in a personal way, including its application, which have and will continue to dilute the outcome of many good-intentioned and sacrificial ministries. This causes God much pain, and restricts His release on earth in this critical hour.

To strategically impact our generation, to open up spiritual realities for future generations, we should adhere to divine, eternal principles. Our primary focus should always be to minister to God in an undiluted, unadulterated way. We build an altar unto Him! He is to be exalted above all!

Why Dwelling Places?

We view the earth in geographical terms: mountains, rivers, deserts, oceans, and recognised nations with clear boundaries. In exactly the same way, the earth can also be seen as a spiritual map with different spiritual markings.

Since the Fall, the earth has been a place of contention between the kingdom of heaven, and the kingdoms of the evil one. All kings want to rule. All kings want to subdue land. Kings do not serve other kingdoms, well not without a big fight.

Luke 4:5-7: *The devil took [Jesus] up and showed Him all the kingdoms of the world in a moment of time, and said to Him, 'To you I will give all this authority and their glory, for it has been delivered to me, and I give it to whom I will. If you, then, will worship me, it will all be yours.'*

Any earthly empire or nation who wants to exercise authority in a territory needs representatives and a physical address within the occupied territory. These headquarters of a particular authority can be a palace, a parliament, military barracks; or even just a beachhead. This physical expression represents a whole system in place that has authority to exercise laws accordingly, and therefore demands obedience throughout this particular region. Whoever is seated in the headquarters has authority over the whole area.

This truth also applies in the spiritual realm. Any spiritual kingdom needs a place on earth from which to function, in order to extend their authority and characteristics; usually called a stronghold.[44] Demonic powers strategically built, established and strengthened strongholds in the nations throughout many millennia. This is their platform from where the evil one exercised authority to enslave mankind, sowing lies, setting traps, bringing about total defilement of the nations, with the intention of Death to rule on earth.

In research and spiritual mapping of continents and nations, we see how strategic places of demonic worship have been protected, destroyed and rebuilt again throughout the ages. For example: the Mayan civilization in South America, Babylon in Persia, pagan places of worship in Turkey and Greece, as well as pagan sites in Greenland, Ireland and Mongolia. 'Gods' and 'goddesses' often underwent a name-change through the ages and in a different context, such as the Greek Zeus who is also known as the Roman Jupiter, and the Babylonian Ishtar who has also been identified as Tamuz, Astarte and Venus in different empires. Despite this name change, the demonic power remains unchanged, functioning from within the same strongholds, demanding idolatrous worship that is to be offered from generation to generation.

Worship of these entities is necessary to continuously exercise authority over a certain people and territory on earth. If

---

44   Judges 9:47,49; 1Samuel 23:14; 1Chronicles 11.7; Mark 3:27

the worship dwindles, then their authority also dissipates. Thus, their headquarters are often built on high places, on strategic crossings of lay lines, or in the centre of societies.[45] These temples and ancient sites have remained throughout the ages to be spiritually open portals in the heavenlies for demonic powers to travel, manifest and exercise control over the next generation, always demanding sacrificial worship. Using the constellations of stars and underground water channels, these demonic strongholds have established a demonic web across the nations. Looking down on the spiritual map of the earth, it is as if the evil forces were spinning an increasingly thickening web over the nations to keep the light out, to darken the understanding of nations, and prevent spiritual revelation and salvation of individuals, as well as the transformation of nations. This is a satanic strategy orchestrated over many generations.

2Corinthians 3:14-16: *But their minds were blinded. For to this day, when they read the old covenant, that same veil remains unlifted, because only through Christ is it taken away. Yes, to this day whenever Moses is read a veil lies over their hearts. But when one turns to the Lord, the veil is removed.*

Satan is unable to come up with any of his own strategies to have lasting effects. He always copies the ways of God in twisted deception, with selfish purposes. Consequently, these demonic forces use the same spiritual principles to build, just as the King Eternal does. The enemy understood these eternal principles and laid claim to them to strengthen his own rulership on earth. In establishing a place of consistent worship and sacrifice, he paves the way for

---

45.   George Otis Jnr.: *Informed Intercession (2001).*
Also by the same author: *The Twilight labyrinth. (1997)*

the eventual manifestation of the authority and rulership of a particular demonic entity. From such a stronghold, just as with a military base, this demonic power can exercise certain authority to serve his lord, Lucifer. Once headquarters are established, the evil power will continue to demand worship and obedience from the people, usually through fear, guilt, deception and manipulation. Over time, obedience to this power becomes part of the culture of the people, a permanent imprint in their personality. To go against this in any culture, brings about much confrontation and opposition. Unless there is clear vision of the spiritual strategy in the heavenlies, these unseen battles can become too intense to overcome, and we succumb to fit into our surroundings, doing life just as the others do. After all, spiritual kingdoms demand submission.

Once authority has been firmly established, and worship is an ongoing reality, the spirit can spread its nets to nearby lands and peoples with similar or slightly different ways, but always with the same intention of ruling over the people and enslaving their minds and emotions, including the next generation.

These realities do not just function through idolatrous temples and pagan practices. Secular universities teaching humanistic philosophies blind the minds and souls of a generation, and many young Christian youth lose their faith in Christ once they start to study, giving in to immorality and alcohol misuse, even drugs. Other demonic strongholds where evil is always obeyed are brothels, gambling houses and shopping malls, not to mention the world-wide-web. In all these mentioned we notice the addictive behaviour where man cannot resist, but sheepishly go along with the crowd. It takes super-human strength to stand against what everybody else is considering as normal.

Islam has successfully followed these essential spiritual principles to strengthen its hold in Muslim nations, and to break new ground in other nations. Wherever Muslims migrate, they always negotiate a physical place for its followers to worship, taking their shoes off and bowing down to their god in a regular, disciplined way. Their daily worship, with weekly and annual festivals, is an unseen spiritual altar. Over time they would press for permission to build a permanent place of worship – a tent, and request the right to call loudly to prayer over the nearby residences. Thus, the stronghold grows in authority in the spiritual realm, always with the intention of spreading its net wider over society, even into government. European nations, with our tolerant and inclusive ideologies, are blindly surrendering our Christian heritages to honour the foreigner, without much spiritual discernment.

These spiritual principles are recognisable in the prostitution networks in cities, and on the internet. It lures and manipulates emotions, deceives the mind; and once trapped, people become slaves for decades, leading to broken families, which destroys the next generation. In the business sector we are constantly being lured to invest and risk, to increase wealth in greedy ways, until it forces a fake identity upon us. We are never satisfied. Once trapped, we keep coming back to 'worship' at the same altar that always demands more.

We recognise the same spiritual principles in Hinduism, neo-paganism, Wicca, and even in Buddhism, albeit in subtler ways, although not less effective.

The evil one implements these spiritual principles to strengthen and extend his own kingdom of darkness in the nations. AND he strategically blinds the followers of Christ to these powerful principles. The result is a generation of casual Christians whose worship is deeply self-centred, longing for personal blessings and favour. Many honest and precious believers build ministries following their own strategies, their own creativity, or copying from others' seemingly successful ministries. We build according to our personalities, our gifts, our financial abilities, even our feelings. We don't have clear priorities in our days, and crisis often demand our immediate attention.

This all leads to exhausted people bearing little fruit. And the little fruit is easily stolen.

Of course, Christians are not completely unaware of these spiritual principles, but we are naïve and ignorant about just how powerful they are. These were originally entrusted to the people of God. It is our inheritance. Our responsibility.

If church communities are ignorant of how to host God's presence in their midst in everlasting ways as a King, the wider society remains locked up for the work of the Holy Spirit to bring revelation and restoration.

Royal Priesthood

You are a chosen generation, a royal priesthood,
a holy nation, a people for possession,
so that you might speak of the praises of Him
who has called you out of darkness
into His marvellous light.

Exodus 19:6

The topic of callings has become an overgrown jungle in our times, and is in great need of being pruned back to its core. It is a word widely used, generally interpreted according to personal preference or circumstantial opinion, often without theological foundations. If our understanding of callings is not rooted in eternity – what has gone before us, and what will come after us once we leave the ministry - then our fruit cannot last forever. All of our business and travel, preaching and social networking, will be tested by fire on the last day.

1Corinthians 3:13-15: *Each one's work will become manifest, for the Day will disclose it, because it will be revealed by fire, and the fire will test what sort of work each one has done. If the work that anyone has built on the foundation survives, he will receive a reward. If anyone's work is burned up, he will suffer loss, though he himself will be saved, but only as through fire.*

Our thinking is regularly individualistic and short-sighted, influenced by humanistic psychology, shaped by our culture. We can't afford not to discern if our calling will produce fruit that endure forever. In the same epistle, apostle Paul exhorts us to build to last:

1Corinthians 3:12-13: *Now if anyone builds on the foundation with gold, silver, precious stones, wood, hay, straw— each one's work will become manifest, for the Day will disclose it, because it will be revealed by fire, and the fire will test what sort of work each one has done.*

The question is simply: how do we build then? What materials do we use to build the Kingdom of God on earth? Any building project requires architectural drawings, a clear vison of the end product. What building methods will we use?

In modern day theology, callings are often classified in the categories of the gifts of the Spirit, as found in **1Corinthians 12:8-10**. It sounds something like: I have an apostolic gift. I am a prophet. I am doing evangelism. I am a pastor.

These are practical, external outworkings of God's calling on our lives to serve Him.

However, prior to the outpouring of the Holy Spirit, and especially in the book of Revelation, God expressed His eternal ways and purposes on earth through a different calling. In the eschaton we will not introduce ourselves to our fellow heavenly members as a lawyer, a nurse, or a missionary. These titles that give us so much identity and security today are extremely temporary.

Eternity seems to have a different view on callings, and that is how we actually will all be measured.

Created for a Purpose

In the Garden of Eden, Adam was created as a **Priest-King**. This humbling grace of being formed and shaped in His image enabled man to worship God in orderly adoration and love. We were not foreign to God, to worship from a distance. There was a similarity between man and God, and yet an otherworldly distance. There was inclusion, and yet a fearful reverence. There was friendship, and yet a knowledge that He is infinite.

Mankind found his identity in God, and was satisfied and fulfilled in God. Adam could see, to a limited extent, who and what he could become if he continued to develop and grow into the fullness of what God had in store for mankind on earth. Worshipping God was Adam's highest calling, the only reality that completely satisfied him.

God is King

1Timothy 1:17: *To the King of the ages, immortal, invisible, the only God, be honour and glory forever and ever. Amen.*

If we are created in His image, then we can conclude that God created Adam and Eve to rule on earth, as an extension of His heavenly kingdom. Like any true king, Adam was endowed with glory and honour, as well as authority.

Psalm 8:5: *Yet you have made him a little lower than the heavenly beings, and crowned him with glory and honour.*

Adam's authority as king on earth was intended to bring life to the entire cosmos, rooted firmly in his worship of, and fellowship with the Lord as a priest. These were the conditions for God's heavenly authority to flow through the earthly priest and establish prosperity and peace for all of creation. Outside of worship and obedience, man had no authority in himself to rule on earth.

Jesus would later describe this priestly kingship in great simplicity in **Matthew 22:37-39:** *You shall love the Lord your God with all your heart and with all your soul and with all your mind. This is the great and first commandment. And a second is like it: You shall love your neighbour as yourself.*

These vertical and horizontal axes, these heavenly and earthly dimensions formed the foundation of man's calling: To love the Lord our God, and to love our neighbour.

This is not an option of either/or. We were created to walk in the fullness of both. This is the mandate of man on earth. The perfection of a humble stance before the Great I Am endows mankind with heavenly authority to be a blessing to animals, birds, fish and life in general. The one reveals the other. These are not two sides of the same coin. They are one – an expression of God's heart and purpose for all mankind: In worship, one's life is saturated with awe for the Creator, who rules through the worshipper for His glory and purposes on earth. This Priest-King brings life to our earthly planet.

In chapter 6, we will see how Adam was created as King, and in chapter 7 we will look at the Priesthood of Adam.

The Fall, and the calling of Priest-King

After the Fall in Eden, this heavenly calling was torn apart and buried in fear and shame. The two offices of priest and king were separated from each other, and distorted in unprecedented ways to the point that we have barely any insight in any of it today. We lost nearly all insight and comprehension of the divine union of these offices. Today, the topic of priest-king is both baffling and daunting, and we know of few people who live it out in its prophetic fullness. This concept, this everlasting calling, got nearly lost throughout time, stolen, as we grapple in church with wide-spread clerical corruption, a seemingly increasingly irrelevant priesthood; diluted, soulish worship practices on one side, or dry routine on the other side.

To bring these two aspects of priest and king together with force brought about much confusion and shame to the Body of Christ throughout history, and we feel safe in keeping them desperately apart. Authority is for government. Priesthood is for the church domain, a calling to serve.

How sad is the acceptance of our brokenness, our poverty.
How huge the consequences in society, and for our planet.

Old Testament Examples

The function of a priest, the representative of religious life,
is distinctly different from that of being king, the leader of
civil life in a nation. The fullness of heavenly authority on
earth was only restored in the New Testament in the life of
Jesus. And yet, God in faithfulness presents us with several
examples of these two expressions in the Old Testament.
There were periods when these offices functioned together,
serving each other, especially in the God-fearing seasons
in Israel. Although these offices functioned alongside each
other, they were not united within one person, but rather
worked through different parties. During the apostate
seasons of Israel, these offices would be even further
separated, often directly opposing each other. Let's look at
some examples:

Melchizedek

The first time the city of Jerusalem is mentioned in the Bible
is in association with the name of its king, Melchizedek.
A few mystical verses in **Genesis chapter 14** give us a
small peek into eternity. In this unknown king we see the
manifestation of the office of king and priest in one person,
manifesting in his wise rulership on earth. His life is an
exception – a prophetic proclamation of what was to come.

We read that Abraham triumphed in battle over several
kings who had taken his cousin Lot captive. In **Genesis
14:17-24** the King of Salem came to meet Abraham.
Salem is geographically the present-day Jerusalem, and

prophetically speaks of the city of God, the Place of Peace (*Shalom* in Hebrew*).*

Psalm 76:2: *His abode is in Salem; and His dwelling place in Zion.*

King Melchizedek was a high-priest of God Most High (v.18). He blessed Abraham and served the patriarch bread and wine, foreshadowing the sacrifice of Christ. Abram paid a tithe of everything to this priestly king, although in coming centuries tithes were always presented to the priests.

Hebrews 7:1-4: *For this Melchizedek, king of Salem and priest of the Most High God, met Abraham returning from the slaughter of the kings and blessed him. To him Abraham also gave a tenth of all. He was first by interpretation king of righteousness, and after that also king of Salem, which is king of peace, without father, without mother, without descent, having neither beginning of days nor end of life, but made like the Son of God, he remains a priest continually. Now consider how great this man was, to whom even the patriarch Abraham gave the tenth of the spoils.*

Melchizedek's kingship was one of Righteousness and Peace, and his people prospered with honour and dignity. This is only made possible through a life of constant worship to the heavenly King.

Melchizedek is the only example in whom these offices functioned fruitfully in one person. In all other examples we will see these offices functioning separately, in different people.

✝ **Moses** was the fatherly authority in Israel, whilst **Aaron** was the high priest.

† The tribe of **Judah** was considered to be leaders in Israel: **Genesis 49:8:** *Judah, your brothers shall praise you; …your father's sons shall bow down before you.*

The tribe of **Levi** served God and Israel in the temple: **Deuteronomy 10:8:** *At that time the LORD set apart the tribe of Levi to carry the ark of the covenant of the LORD to stand before the LORD to minister to Him and to bless in His Name, to this day.*

† **Samuel** was a priest judging the nation of Israel, while first **Saul** and later **David** were anointed to be kings.[46] King Saul was initially open for, and dependent on the advice and authority of the priest Samuel, but he quickly turned away and functioned independently, even crossing the divine boundary lines to present unlawful priestly sacrifices himself, without waiting on Samuel.[47] This act of rebellious independence led to God rejecting Saul as king. The priesthood is holy unto God, and nobody can simply step into this role by his own choice. Priests are appointed by God alone.[48]

† In the book of Nehemiah, whilst the walls of Jerusalem were being rebuilt, **Zerubbabel** acted as the governor – the civil leader, whilst **Joshua** was the high priest.[49] They worked closely together, and we don't read about any confusion in their independent roles. Under their leadership, the work flourished and was completed within fifty-two days.

---

46.   1Samuel 7:15-17
47.   1Samuel 13
48.   Hebrews 5:1
49.   Haggai 1:1?

The Messiah as Priest-King

Reuniting these two offices in Jesus was foretold in the Old Testament.

Zechariah 6:9-14: *The Word of God came to me saying, … take silver and gold, and make crowns, and set them on the head of Joshua the son of Jehozadak, the high priest. Speak to him, saying, so speaks the Lord of Hosts, saying, Behold the Man whose name is The Branch! He shall spring up out of His place, and He shall build the temple of the LORD. Even He shall build the temple of the LORD; and He shall bear the glory, and shall sit and rule on His throne. He shall be a priest on His throne; and the counsel of peace shall be between them both.*

Crowns are kingly attire, and yet it was prepared for the high priest?! Thrones are symbols of kingly authority, and not symbolic of the priesthood?! Zachariah proclaims here that Jesus shall be a priest on His throne. The priestly kingship shall be restored on earth, united and functioning within a single human being.

In Christ, these two everlasting offices were restored in one person, according to God's everlasting ways. Jesus is, was, and will always be the eternal **King**, enthroned in heaven and earth. He was king before creation, throughout the Old Testament, openly declared in the New Testament, and fulfilled in the End Times, until all eternity.

Daniel 7:13-14: *I saw in the night visions, and behold, with the clouds of heaven there came one like a son of man, and He came to the Ancient of Days and was presented before Him. And to Him was given dominion and glory and a kingdom, that all peoples, nations, and languages should serve Him; His dominion is an everlasting dominion, which shall not pass away, and His kingdom one that shall not be destroyed.*

Revelation 19:11,16: *Then I saw heaven opened, and behold, a white horse! The One sitting on it is called Faithful and True, and in righteousness He judges and makes war...On His robe and on His thigh He has a Name written, King of kings and Lord of lords.*

In **Psalm two** we read that all authority of the nations is restored to Jesus as the only begotten Son of God, the Son of Man, even from the moment of His Incarnation.

Psalm 2:6-11: *As for Me, I have set my King on Zion, My holy hill. I will tell of the decree: The LORD said to Me, 'You are my Son; today I have begotten you. Ask of Me, and I will make the nations your heritage, and the ends of the earth your possession. You shall break them with a rod of iron and dash them in pieces like a potter's vessel.' Now therefore, O kings, be wise; be warned, O rulers of the earth. Serve the LORD with fear, and rejoice with trembling.*

Jesus was, is and will always be our **High Priest** according to an order superior to that of Aaron. He is a High Priest in the order of Melchizedek.[50]

For generations the high priest was ordained according to the Levitical law, a priest who offered sacrifices first for his own sins, and then on behalf of his people. These high priests served for the period of their lifetime, and had to be replaced by another after their death.

But not Jesus. His priesthood is based on heavenly authority, rather than on lineage.

Hebrews 7:16,23-24: *Who has become a priest, not on the basis of a legal requirement concerning bodily descent, but by the power of an indestructible life. The former priests were many in*

---

50. Hebrews 7:11 22

number, because they were prevented by death from continuing in office, but He holds His priesthood permanently, because He continues forever.

The Levites entered the priesthood as an inheritance due to their bloodline. But Jesus was from the regal tribe of Judah, and none from Judah ever served as priests. They had to offer sacrifices for their own sins daily, and annually, according to the pattern given to Moses on Mount Sinai. Jesus made His perfect sacrifice only once, gaining eternal redemption for all who come to God by faith through Jesus.

Hebrews 9:12: *Nor by the blood of goats and calves, but by His own blood He entered once for all into the Holies, having obtained eternal redemption for us.*

Jesus was sinless and had no need to offer a sacrifice for Himself, as did the priests of the Old Testament. Rather than a yearly atonement, Jesus' sacrifice is once-for-all,[51] an eternal, divine sacrifice that continues to work powerfully for all eternity. Jesus' priesthood is a heavenly reality that manifested on earth, not a temporary, earthly responsibility.

With Jesus as High Priest, a new covenant came into effect. Jesus' priesthood institutes a new beginning for all times.

Hebrews 7:12: *For when there is a change in the priesthood, there is necessarily a change in the law as well.*

Jesus fulfilled each aspect of the old Aaronic order, and is proclaimed High Priest forever in the order of Melchizedek, who was both king and priest.[52] Jesus became man, was subject to all our weaknesses, passions and temptations,

---

51. Hebrews 10:1-18
52. Hebrews 6:20

yet without ever submitting to sin.[53] He entered into Hades, and served there as High Priest, through the perfect sacrifice of His own body and blood. He became the substitute sacrifice who died, the ransom who paid all the debts of our deserved judgement. He destroyed death. He now rules in heaven in His royal priesthood at the heavenly altar[54], in justice, righteousness and mercy.

The Church

Through the covenant of salvation, believers are grafted into Christ by grace. The restoration which Jesus prepared for all mankind in His sacrifice and victory over sin and death on the cross includes the restoration of the office of Priest-King on earth for all believers. In Christ, believers are called to a higher calling as David, or Aaron. We are called to be both priests and kings, not one or the other. These are not separate offices, but one. As the authority on earth has been regained in Christ and given to believers, we are to bring His authority as kings on earth as we continually minister as priests to the King of all ages. Priest-kings pray with authority for the nations.

In **1Peter 2:9** God reaffirms His everlasting heart's intention to the New Testament Church as He did when He first brought the Israelites out of slavery in **Exodus 19:6**. The Holy Spirit uses just about the exact same words, proclaiming the eternal intention of God's heart:

But you are a chosen generation, a royal priesthood, a holy nation, a people for possession, so that you might speak of the praises of Him who has called you out of darkness into His marvellous light.

---

53. Hebrews 4:15
54. Revelation 8:3; 9:13

In the redemption, through the death, resurrection and ascension of Christ, this magnificent Priestly Kingship was restored to mankind who are redeemed by His life. Each individual who is in a covenantal relationship with Jesus is called to walk in this ancient, superior calling, as Adam was intended to. This is not by our own preference, but rather a responsibility given from heaven.

To exercise God's authority on earth, we have to minister in the heavenly places to the King of kings. Our kingly authority is rooted in the fact that Jesus restored us to the Godhead in heaven. Therefore, we can stand before His throne in adoration, and truly bring life to earth, as intended in **Genesis chapter one**. In the resurrection and ascension of Jesus, the heavenlies have been opened for us, even the Most Holy Place, as the curtain was torn in His resurrection. In the ascension of Christ, we are raised up and seated in Christ in the heavenly places, first to be priests in the heavenlies unto God, and also to bring His life to nations in His authority that works through us.

Hebrews 8:1: *We have such a High Priest, who has sat down on the right of the throne of the Majesty in Heaven.*

Ephesians 2:6: *...and raised us up with Him and seated us with Him in the heavenly places in Christ Jesus.*

In Kingly authority our High Priest rules over all – the Lamb seated on the throne.[55] Our King is our eternal Servant who laid down His life for all. His authority does not oppress, but restores the fallen and broken to dignity and glory. His throne is the source of our authority in the nations. We can never rule in our own authority, or in our own ways. Our position and calling to rule with authority can never be

---

55.   Revelation 5:13

independent from the sacrifice of the Lamb who saved us from death and the miry clay. Our authority to rule on earth is directly related to how much King Jesus rules and reigns within our own hearts

This calling of priest-kings is not given to a superior few, whilst the rest are to form the congregation of passive followers. In Christ, each believer is restored and called to be a priestly king, a royal priest. From this eternal calling, all fruitfulness sprouts in the Kingdom of God.

Without entering into the fullness of this calling, our fruit will not last the testing of eternal fire. I may go as far as to say that, without fulfilling this calling, we can never glorify God in heaven, or on earth. There is only one way, and it is His original, everlasting way. This is confirmed in the book of Revelation:

Revelation 1:6: *[He] made us kings and priests to God and His Father, to Him be glory and dominion forever and ever. Amen.*

Revelation 5:10: *You made us kings and priests to our God, and we will reign over the earth.*

Revelation 20:6: *Blessed and holy is he who has part in the first resurrection. The second death has no authority over these, but they will be priests of God and of Christ, and will reign with Him a thousand years.*

As we gaze through heavenly windows into distant eternity, we find in the crowds surrounding His throne no teachers, lawyers or humanitarian workers. All will be known according to the fulfilment of His perfect, everlasting ways, if we completed our earthly journey as priest-kings.

Have we been priestly kings in our generation?

This calling of priest-king does not automatically come into effect in a conversion experience. Although it is given to us in Christ, we need to grow in discipline and maturity, to discover and unlock the fullness of this calling in Christ.

Blessed is the man/woman to whom it is given to recognise that this is the ultimate theme in the Bible – to represent the King of kings on earth through continuous worship and priestly liturgy. Much fruit will be entrusted to such a person who humbly worships God as his primary purpose on earth.

Adamic Kingship

*Yet you have made him a little lower than the heavenly beings
and crowned him with glory and honour.
You have given him dominion over the works of your hands;
you have put all things under his feet.*

Psalm 8:5,6

The garden of Eden was a mystical place in which God's eternal purposes for mankind were originally proclaimed. Eden was the earthly headquarters of the heavenly kingdom, an earthly temple for the Eternal God. This topic is filled with revelation. Different streams of theology throughout the ages have produced a variety of views on creation. What follows is a fragment of the teachings of the Church Fathers from the first four centuries.

Ruler on Earth

Genesis 1:26: *Then God said, 'Let us make man in our image, after our likeness. Let them have dominion over the fish of the sea and over the birds of the heavens and over the livestock and over all the earth and over every creeping thing that creeps on the earth.'*

Genesis 1:28: *God blessed them. And God said to them, 'Be fruitful and multiply and fill the earth and subdue it, and have dominion over the fish of the sea and over the birds of the heavens and over every living thing that moves on the earth.'*

God placed Adam in Eden, and gave him the special commission to tend and keep the land as king on earth. Every tiny aspect of God's creation was created with a purpose. God gradually taught Adam to perceive the divine purpose of each animal, commissioning him to name each creature accordingly. The lion, for example, with its loud roar and feline characteristics, was created to carry out a specific role that is different from other creatures. This process of naming the identity of each of the animals reinforced their purpose in creation. The animals came alive in who they were created to be, with growing trust and enjoyment between man and the animal world.

Genesis 2:19-20: *Now out of the ground the LORD God had formed every beast of the field and every bird of the heavens and brought them to the man to see what he would call them. And whatever the man called every living creature, that was its name. The man gave names to all livestock and to the birds of the heavens and to every beast of the field.*

What a joy for Adam to perceive God's perfect, everlasting intentions for the earth, a journey of discovery and adventure as Adam fellowshipped with God, growing in his role and responsibility on earth. God was fathering Adam as he was finding his feet as ruler on earth. This relationship between God and Adam brought Life and Peace to all created beings, from the tiniest ant, to the brightest cockatoo. It was a tender and exiting process, filled with awe and sense of the future of the earth, the Kingdom of God.

This kingly commission of Adam contains manifold eternal mysteries which will be fulfilled in the eschaton, at the return of Christ to reign on earth.

Eden

We should consider the Hebrew meaning of the word *Eden*, as it was the beginning of all, the foundation to all history. *Eden* means 'a place of worship,' or 'a place of delight'. It was a holy place filled with joyful pleasure, an earthly temple described as 'delicate', in which God dwelt with man, and in man. This word is closely connected to the Hebrew term for 'heaven' or 'paradise', which denotes a place saturated with the presence of God.

Eden was the first place on planet earth where God's presence dwelt within human beings, from where the

Kingdom of God on earth was unfolding, as heaven and earth was one unit.

In God's instruction to Adam to tend and keep the garden, He uses the same Hebrew word used a few centuries later to consecrate Aaron as priest to serve in the tabernacle, to stand before God on behalf of the nations.[56]

Genesis 2:15: *The LORD God took the man and put him in the garden of Eden to work it and keep it.*

Leviticus 8:35: *You shall remain at the door of the tabernacle of the congregation day and night seven days, and keep the charge of LORD, so that you do not die, for so I have commanded.*

To 'keep and tend' is a priestly function to watch over the glory of God, maintaining the flow of divine life from heaven to earth. This is the necessary condition for man to experience heavenly authority on earth, securing prosperity to all creation. Eden was indeed heaven on earth. And God's Kingdom manifested for complete *shalom*[57] of the whole earth.

Isaiah 43:21: *This people I have formed for Myself; they shall declare My praise.*

In worshipping God, Adam was to train all creation to worship with him, bringing creation into greater revelation and knowledge of God. This delightful fellowship between God and Adam was a continuous source of life for the whole cosmos. This is symbolised in the presence of the

---

56. Strong's Concordance: **H8104** *shâmar* - to *hedge* about (as with thorns), that is, *guard*; to *protect, attend to*, etc.: beware, be circumspect, take heed, keep, mark, look narrowly, observe, preserve, regard, reserve, save, sure, to be a watchman.
57. Strong's Concordance: **H796** *shâlôm* - safe, that is well, happy, friendly; also welfare, health, prosperity, peace.

Tree of Life in the midst of the Garden, and the River of Life which flows out to the rest of the earth, releasing heavenly blessing to all creatures and creation, everlasting life, favour and goodness to earth.

The nature of this fellowship was love. God gave all of Himself to Adam, and man was filled and satisfied, body, soul and spirit.

Genesis 2:7: *Then the LORD God formed the man of dust from the ground and breathed into his nostrils the breath of life, and the man became a living creature.*

This fellowship brought pleasure to God.

Proverbs 8:31: *Rejoicing in His inhabited world and delighting in the children of man.*

This vertical axis between heaven and earth is the horizontal platform for authority and dominion over the birds, seas and all living beings. The one cannot exist without the other. Authority outside of humble worship never brings life.

The Tree of Knowledge of Good and Evil

This is a disputed topic with variable interpretations. The early church Fathers were clear in their teaching on this tree.

Genesis 2:8-10: *God planted a garden eastward in Eden. There He put the man whom He had formed. And out of the ground God caused to grow every tree that is pleasant to the sight, and good for food. The Tree of Life also was in the middle of the garden, and the Tree of knowledge of good and evil. And a river went out of Eden to water the garden. From there it was divided and became four heads.*

In God's loving protection of Eden, this state of perfection, God established clear boundaries. He knew of the envious enemy who could not bear divine love and life, craving worship for himself, having previously lost his place in heaven due to prideful self-exaltation.

Genesis 2:16-17: *The LORD God commanded man, saying, 'You may surely eat of every tree of the garden, but of the tree of the knowledge of good and evil you shall not eat, for in the day that you eat of it you shall surely die.'*

Yet, lamentably, Adam and Eve were not watchful, and were deceived by the serpent.

Before we try to answer the question about the Evil Tree in the midst of Garden of Eden, we should first understand the place of Lucifer in the Garden.

In **Ezekiel 28:11-28** we read: *You were in Eden, the garden of God...* Scholars agree that this scripture refers to the fallen cherub, called Lucifer. We find certain characteristics in this passage describing the archangel before his fall, while he was orchestrating a host of angels in praise before the throne of God. This passage corresponds with **Isaiah chapter 14**, which also describes Lucifer. The early Church Fathers taught that there were two personalities in the Garden of Eden at the time when Adam was created. This truth needs to be unfolded, otherwise we will not grow in our understanding of prayer for our own generation to see God's Kingdom on earth.

God created Lucifer, as He created all angelic orders.

Nehemiah 9:6: *You are the LORD, You alone. You have made heaven, the heaven of heavens, with all their host, the earth and all that is on it, the seas and all that is in them; and You preserve all of them; and the host of heaven worships You.*

Colossians 1:16: *For by Him all things were created, in heaven and on earth, visible and invisible, whether thrones or dominions or rulers or authorities – all things were created through Him and for Him.*

In creation, God appointed the cherub Lucifer, the head of the angelic ranks, to be prince of the earth. In **Luke 4:6** Satan says to Jesus during His temptation in the wilderness, that all authority on earth has been given to him. Jesus even calls Lucifer in **John 14:13** the 'prince of this world,' although he had no authority over Jesus.

We also know that God gave the authority of the earth to Adam.

Psalm 115:16: *The heavens are the Lord's, but earth He has given to the sons of men.*

How can we explain this possible contradiction? What authority was given to the cherub? And what authority was given to Adam?

There is a clear, eternal order in God's mind. This mystery has been lost through the ages, but was taught and manifested in the Early Church. Understanding God's mind from the beginning, will open up for us in greater depth the life and sacrifice of Jesus to bring salvation and restoration, and it will equip us to hasten His Second Coming when His Eternal order will again manifest on earth in its full glory as was intended in Genesis one.

God never intended heaven and earth to be separate entities. They were created in a seamless way, both serving the Kingdom of God. God created the angelic hosts first, being given their place in the heavenlies with a unique heavenly ministry. In time, Adam was created on the sixth day, and was put in the garden of Eden to rule and reign on earth. There was a time lapse between these two creations.

God's eternal intention was that these two creations would be working closely together on earth: one with heavenly features suited for the heavenlies, and the other with a material nature suitable for earth. This synergistic relationship would bring creation to its full, eternal potential, to host the King in His glory on earth. This is a key principle to understand in how to establish His Kingdom on earth in prayer and ministry.

I repeat myself: It was God's intent from the beginning that heavenly, angelic beings would serve and work closely with mankind for eternal, Kingdom purposes on earth.[58]

The fall disrupted even the heavenlies. Adam was cut off from the heavens and the angels. Since the fall, we find the cherub and his angels at war with mankind, instead of serving in synergy.

How Did the Fall Come About?

Was this cherub already fallen by the time Adam was created? Did Lucifer have access to the garden of Eden? If all authority on earth was given to Adam, where did Lucifer's authority come from? These are big questions.

Ezekiel 28:13-15: *You were in Eden, the garden of God; every precious stone was your covering, sardius, topaz, and diamond, beryl, onyx, and jasper, sapphire, emerald, and carbuncle; and crafted in gold were your settings and your engravings. On the day that you were created they were prepared. You were an*

---

58.   Ephesians 1:9-10

anointed guardian cherub. I placed you; you were on the holy mountain of God; in the midst of the stones of fire you walked. You were blameless in your ways from the day you were created, till unrighteousness was found in you.

How astonishing that the Garden of Eden was the place assigned to Lucifer before his fall. This was his domain to serve mankind in obedience to God. The same garden became Adam's residence when he was created, the place where he was commissioned to reign on earth.

Genesis 2:15: *The LORD God took the man and put him in the garden of Eden.*

God's intent was that Adam and Lucifer would minister together in this united earthly-and-heavenly-realm. Just to underline again, that in the minds of Adam and Lucifer there was only one unit – not two vastly different domains. Heaven and Earth was one, created to hold and proclaim His glory in all eternity.

The cherub would be the prince of the heavenly orders over the earth; and Adam the prince on earth. Two creatures with different features and personalities: angelic and human, were to serve together in God's Kingdom to reflect God's life, light, beauty, wisdom and goodness. Together they would lead the nations on earth towards God's eternal purposes.

The angel was created first and was put in Eden. As he was assigned to serve closely with Adam, we can expect the cherub's calling to be similar to Adam's. The cherub was to serve Adam in his priestly role, and was therefore created to be a worshipper, a musical instrument. Lucifer was intended to minister with Adam in leading all creation into structured, holy adoration of the eternal King.

And yet, we know that all of creation was created with free will. Even this cherub had a choice. The cherub jealously craved worship for himself. This arrogant, self-centred desire was the seed of evil that entered into creation.

Isaiah 14:12-15: *How you are fallen from heaven, O Day Star, son of Dawn! How you are cut down to the ground, you who laid the nations low! You said in your heart, 'I will ascend to heaven; above the stars of God I will set my throne on high; I will sit on the mount of assembly in the far reaches of the north; I will ascend above the heights of the clouds; I will make myself like the Most High.' But you are brought down to Sheol, to the far reaches of the pit.*

Lucifer lost his place in the heavens, and also his heavenly assignment. He was cast down to the earth.

Revelation 12:7-10: *Now war arose in heaven, Michael and his angels fighting against the dragon. And the dragon and his angels fought back, but he was defeated, and there was no longer any place for them in heaven. And the great dragon was thrown down, that ancient serpent, who is called the devil and Satan, the deceiver of the whole world—he was thrown down to the earth, and his angels were thrown down with him.*

The cherub was created with rich knowledge and insight[59] - covered in eyes, to know. According to the writings of the Church fathers in the early centuries, this cherub knew God's intention of another creature in the garden who would reign on earth. Sin always breeds sin. This seed of jealous superiority within Lucifer developed into an evil determination to cast mankind out from Eden, the headquarters of the Kingdom. When Adam was created on the sixth day, he was placed in Eden with authority to rule

---

59.   Ezekiel 28:12ᶜ

on earth. The cherub was furious, and from this point on the battle between mankind and the fallen angel started. This enemy of humanity would seek to tempt Adam. The same poison that made Lucifer fall[60] was used in this planned temptation of Adam:

Genesis 3:1-5: *Now the serpent was more crafty than any other beast of the field that the LORD God had made. He said to the woman, 'Did God actually say, 'You shall not eat of any tree in the garden?" And the woman said to the serpent, 'We may eat of the fruit of the trees in the garden, but God said, 'You shall not eat of the fruit of the tree that is in the midst of the garden, neither shall you touch it, lest you die." But the serpent said to the woman, 'You will not surely die. For God knows that when you eat of it your eyes will be opened, and you will be like God, knowing good and evil.'*

How was it even possible for the devil to deceive Adam in such a perfect environment as Eden, especially in the light of God's clear warning about the dangers of the Tree of Knowledge?[61]

The enemy can only copy God's methods, after twisting them in accordance to his own evil nature. Adam was an earthly gardener in the Garden of Eden,[62] *cultivating* the garden, that is to *sow trees*, and to tend all. Lucifer was created as a perfect heavenly match to serve alongside Adam. He had a similar commission as Adam, but in the heavenlies over the earth. Adam was keeping the Garden of Eden, and similarly Lucifer was given the ability to sow spiritual seed[63] – a heavenly gardener. These were

---

60.   Isaiah 14:13-14
61.   Genesis 2:16-17
62.   Genesis 2:15
63.   Matthew 13:24-27

not merely trees to feed our bodies,[64] but as the manna was for Israel, they would nourish the whole being, body, soul and spirit. It was to be the food of heaven, also called angels' food.[65]

Satan used this God-given ability in a selfish way to serve his evil purposes. In **Genesis chapter three**, Satan planted a tree in Eden that bore his own evil nature, to serve his selfish purposes. This was the **Tree of the Knowledge of Good and Evil**. The fruit of this tree was poisonous, although deceptively attractive – a true bait.

Genesis 3:6: *So when the woman saw that the tree was good for food, and that it was a delight to the eyes, and that the tree was to be desired to make one wise, she took of its fruit and ate.*

There is much confusion about the origin of this tree, for its existence as a source of evil seems to contradict the supposed perfection of Eden.

God can never be the source of evil. On the contrary, God warned Adam not to eat of this tree. He is the wise Shepherd, warning us of danger.

James 1:13: *God cannot be tempted by evil, nor does He Himself tempt anyone.*

The origin of this tree is suggested in Jesus' parable of the weeds in **Matthew 13:24–30:**

Vv. 27ᵇ-28: *'Master, did you not sow good seed in your field? How then does it have weeds?' Jesus said to them, 'An enemy has done this.'*

---

64. Genesis 1:29
65. Psalm 78:25

In the same chapter Jesus explains the parable to His disciples:

Vv. 37-39ª: *Jesus answered, 'The one who sows the good seed is the Son of Man. The field is the world, and the good seed is the sons of the kingdom. The weeds are the sons of the evil one, and the enemy who sowed them is the devil.'*

One of the many titles of the devil is 'deceiver'. Since the devil planted this tree himself, and since it was under his authority, the devil used its poisonous fruit which bore his own character – attractive to the eye, deceitful, empty, and leading to death.

Adam and Eve were not watchful,[66] and being deceived, they were driven out of the Garden. Mankind lost his authority, and the enemy seized this inheritance illegally and was afterwards called 'the ruler of this world'.[67] Deceit by definition refers to practices designed to mislead, with intentional misrepresentation of the truth and the Creator. Deceit remains the *modus operandi* of the enemy against Adam and all his future descendants.

2John 1:7: *For many deceivers have gone out into the world.*

The Tree of Life

Thanks be to God, who in His infinite foreknowledge and compassion knew the plans of the enemy against humanity and His kingdom. God prepared in advance the way to nullify the plans of the devil. God Himself planted the Tree of Life in Eden; the fruit of which would be for the salvation

---

66.   Galatians 6:1
67.   John 12:31; 14:30; 16:11

and healing of nations, sweet fruit that would nullify the poisonous fruit of Satan. It was present in the Garden as a mystical proclamation of God's eternal salvation for creation.[68]

After all, Jesus is the everlasting gardener, who watches over us.

Matthew 13:3: *A sower went out to sow.*

In **Ezekiel 47:12** we read that the Tree of Life, planted by the Last Adam, Christ, is for the restoration and redemption of mankind: *On the banks, on both sides of the river, there will grow all kinds of trees for food. Their leaves will not wither, nor their fruit fail, but they will bear fresh fruit every month, because the water for them flows from the sanctuary. Their fruit will be for food, and their leaves for healing.*

If the Fall never happened

Adam would have continued to mature in living out his assignment on earth as king-priest until his time of rest came. He would then have been raised up to the heavenly realm, after completing his role in the earthly realm. We get a glimpse of this knowledge in the lives of Enoch and Elijah, and even more clearly in Christ's transfiguration.

After the Fall

The Fall distorted all perfection and harmony. Man's relationship with God was broken,[69] and the heavens and the earth were separated. Mankind ended up with only a

---

68. 1Peter 1:19b-20
69. Genesis 3:24

horizontal focus, having lost even the memory of a vertical stance before God. We became the main centres of our own lives, in relationship with fellow human beings, working out our existence in our earthly spheres of responsibility.

Our generation is imprisoned in this horizontal realm, and our ministry is often about church fellowship, numerical growth, fundraising, social-networking, and prayer to bless each other. Our desire for the vertical axis is vague, contested and diminishing, and therefore the horizontal fruit becomes increasingly temporary, unable to last the testing of the ages.

We are cut off from the Source of Life. We cannot create Life here on earth of our own good will and works. As the vertical connection is forgotten, even absent, little life-giving authority flows from heaven towards the chaotic earthly realm.

The authority of man on earth can only bring life once a vertical relationship with God enjoys priority over all our horizontal and relational, our earthly responsibilities and callings, even our ministry. We cannot forget that we were created to be priest-kings standing before God first of all.

After the Fall, corruption and distortion prevailed until it reached extortionate dimensions in the time of Noah.[70] After a complete washing away in the flood, once the waters abated and Noah left the ark, we find that Noah immediately built an altar to the Lord, bringing his sacrifices to God.[71] Noah understood that mankind were to be priest-kings. He understood the vertical priority, his priestly calling, to connect heaven and earth.

---

70. Genesis 6
71. Genesis 8:20-22

Genesis 8:20: *Noah built an altar to the LORD and took some of every clean animal and some of every clean bird and offered burnt offerings on the altar.*

God responded to this altar with generous grace and forgiveness. He blessed mankind again in this new beginning on earth with exactly the same blessing He did in creating Adam in the beginning. God even gave Noah the same commissioning as He did to Adam in **Genesis chapter two** to *'be fruitful and multiply and fill the earth'* (**Genesis 9:1**). However, there were some differences between Genesis chapters two and nine. In **Genesis 9:2** onwards it is clear that man's authority over the animals had changed. A fear and dread of human beings seem to prevail in the nature of animals as permission is granted to kill and eat. Death entered the earthly realm, which was never God's intention.

The perimeters of authority which created prosperity and safely for all of creation had been moved. But only temporarily.

The Inheritance Restored in Christ

Contemporary theology would describe the outcomes of the Fall in a general way, primarily as inner, spiritual death, as seen in our separation from God, which demands eternal damnation.[72] In the crucifixion of our Messiah, this judgment was lifted, and man was restored to fellowship with God through Christ, our Mediator.

However, there is more. The key reason Adam was created, God's intention from the start was to give mankind authority on the earth to serve His Kingdom purposes in

---

72.   Romans 3:23

close synergy with the angelic orders, from within a priestly function unto God Himself. Adam lost true priesthood and union with God. And he also lost his authority on earth to rule, his inheritance in the nations.

On the cross Jesus did more than just to solve the problem of sin. Yes, Jesus indeed restored fellowship with God the Father. Moreover, Jesus also opened the way for the potential complete restoration of the original Image of God in mankind.

Romans 8:29[a]: *For those whom He foreknew He also predestined to be conformed to the image of His Son.*

This inner re-creation and restoration of the image of God in mankind comes to its fullness through the ongoing process of working out our salvation in humility and gratitude.[73] In restoring His image in mankind, Jesus also restored the office of Royal Priesthood – to become priest-kings.

It is important to see the connection between the first Adam, and the last Adam. The first Adam was created in God's image.[74] The word *image* is to be an icon of God on earth, to reveal God to the earth. In the fullness of time, Jesus would come as the incarnated God-Man to dwell on earth among man; Immanuel – God with us. He was the exact representation of God, although fully human.

Colossians 1:15: *[Jesus] is the Image of the invisible God, the firstborn of all creation.*

Jesus came as the last Adam[75] to fulfil what the first Adam was unable to complete: to rule on earth.

---

73. Philippians 2:12
74. Genesis 1:27
75. 1Corinthians 15:45

In the incarnation, the voice of the Father speaks through the prophet:

Psalm 2:7-8: *Today I have begotten You; ask of Me and I will give You the nations as Your inherence.*

Jesus' authority manifested openly on every level throughout His ministry. He healed all sicknesses. He delivered those oppressed by demons. He quietened the seas and the wind. He ruled over the fish. He multiplied food and fed the hungry. He never gave in to temptation as He ruled over sin. He entered death, and broke the power of Hades.[76]

When Jesus completely finished His mission on earth, He made a final correction in His resurrection in breathing on the disciples:

John 20:22: *He breathed on them and said to them, 'Receive the Holy Spirit.'*

The word 'breathe' we also find in **Genesis 2:7:** *...and breathed into his nostrils the Breath of Life; and man became a living soul.*

Mankind, flesh and blood, once again has the potential to be filled with the Spirit of God. Eternal Life flowed again into mankind. No longer does death rule in man, or over man. This small group of disciples in the upper room became new Adams with restored authority to rule in union with God on earth. This is clear in Jesus' instruction to the disciples – to rule over sin with authority, and bring life to earth.

---

76. Psalm 21:7 10

John 20:23: *If you forgive the sins of any, they are forgiven them; if you withhold forgiveness from any, it is withheld.*

Jesus' task was fulfilled, and as such He ascended to the Father, and left the new Adams to be icons of Him on earth. These new Adams, this new creation, would represent the Eternal King in the Kingdom of God on earth. The responsibility and commission of believers in having dominion and authority is to preserve the world from chaos – and to direct the world towards God's plan of salvation, even although the world keeps deviating from the ways of God.

Jesus has a vision and desire to restore the world to righteousness and justice. This is why Jesus appoints rulers in the world. The apostles Peter and Paul address this in their letters.[77]

The Church has a great need to understand God's intention in creation, and to restore her responsibility to rule and extend His Kingdom on earth.

Complete Restoration of Heaven and Earth

The full correction and redemption of the destruction caused by the Fall will manifest in the Age to come. Jesus will then restore the unity that existed between the heavenlies and earth, for complete harmony, unity and synergy between the heavenly hosts and human beings.

Colossians 1:19-20: *For in Him all the fullness of God was pleased to dwell, and through Him to reconcile to Himself all things, whether on earth or in heaven, making peace by the blood of His cross.*

---

77.   Romans 14; 1Peter 2

Did the Fall not only affect the earth? What things are not reconciled to Jesus in heaven? Why is it necessary for things in heaven to be reconciled to Jesus? Without doubt, Jesus never died for Lucifer and his fallen angels, and these fallen angels will never be reconciled to God. And the heavenly hosts do not need salvation or restitution, as they have never sinned! So, what are the things apostle Paul is referring to, to be reconciled to God in heaven, assured by the shedding of the blood of Jesus?

Ephesians 1:7-10: *In Him we have redemption through His blood, the forgiveness of our trespasses, according to the riches of His grace, which He lavished upon us, in all wisdom and insight making known to us the mystery of His will, according to His purpose, which He set forth in Christ as a plan for the fullness of time, to unite all things in Him, things in heaven and things on earth.*

These verses refer to the separation between earthly and heavenly orders, the deep disruption and confusion that was caused by the Fall to the perfect order of the divine creation. The Messiah's redemption also addresses and corrects this heavenly destruction to unite the heavenlies and mankind.

This final unity is infinitely more than that which we presently experience in angels serving mankind according to many testimonies in both Testaments, and throughout all history, as angels are ministering agents sent to serve all those on earth.[78] The heavenly reconciliation in the synergistic relationship between angelic hosts and mankind will be completed in His second coming. Now we groan, waiting for the full manifestation of redemption. Presently, the lost inheritance is partially restored, but we await the full manifestation of redemption.

---

78.   Hebrews 1:14

Adamic Priesthood

A chosen generation, a royal priesthood,
a holy nation, His own special people,
that you may proclaim the praises of Him who called you
out of darkness into His marvellous light.

1Peter 2:9

I have often asked friends and colleagues the following question: What is the primary component of being a Priest-King? Is it priesthood? Or kingship? Are we primarily priests with authority to rule in the nations, or are we primarily kings who minister to God?

Sadly, I believe that we are all eager for the authority and power that Jesus has made available to us in His redemption, yet we do not equally long for and value the prerequisite priestly responsibilities and privileges. It is my conviction that in being a Royal Priesthood, our primary calling is to be priests. The word 'royal' is an adjective describing our priesthood. The essence of our calling lies in our ministry to God, ministering in the Holy Place at the heavenly altar, bringing our incense to the throne of grace. The product of priestly faithfulness is royal authority on earth.

Priesthood Responsibility

Priesthood in Eden did not include sacrifices, as sin did not exist. Adam was a priest in its purest form, lifting all his heart, mind and soul to God in love and adoration, carrying all of creation in his heart in teaching creation to worship. Creation was at peace.

Any true priestly calling brings glory to God in heaven, as well as on earth. Priests bring man near to God, into a favourable stance, into actual fellowship. Adam was created to bring all of creation into adoration and growing revelation of their Creator.

Neither Aaron, nor the Levitical priesthood, were able to accomplish this responsibility in its fullness, as they served an inferior priesthood.

Priesthood in the Old Testament

We find two major components of Priesthood mirrored in the physical architecture of the tabernacle and the temple.

The Outer Court

The outer court was the most spacious area in the tabernacle. It was not covered, and was exposed to natural light, referring to the natural and material realm. It was the busy section where Israel, including the foreigners in their midst, brought multiple sets of offerings, even daily. In the outer court the priests tended to the needs of the people. This place was crowded, with priests carrying water, chopping wood, killing sacrifices and letting them bleed out, skinning and gutting sacrifices, and laying them on the brazen altar. Some parts were taken outside the temple courts to be burnt; others were taken into the priestly courts to be eaten. Many detailed instructions were adhered to, depending on the need, or the feast. In the outer court, all priestly service was demanded by, and directed at the people of God. Priests were available to listen and to pray, to bring healing and deliverance, to sprinkle with blood and holy water, to preach and teach.

The outer court symbolises the arena where men and women throughout the ages worked for His kingdom and kingdom principles in righteous ways. Those in government who labour for righteousness and justice, those in the media who stand for truth and community, those who offer counselling and deliverance, cooking soup for the homeless, caring for orphans and strangers, others fighting for sanitation and health. In the outer court, prayer reaches out to nations in intercession, and it speaks up for the voiceless and oppressed. Each act in the outer court, filled with love and faith, is ministry to fellow man and human needs, in obedience and faith to God. Man comes before God to encounter His grace and wisdom, His forgiveness and healing. Ministry in this quarter happens on a horizontal level, having a relational and human focus, to love your neighbour.

In the Old Testament, priests served the Israelites by bringing their sacrifices to God. **Romans 12:1** calls us all to offer all of our bodies as holy sacrifices to God daily, presenting our best and all to Him in gratitude: *I appeal to you therefore, brothers, by the mercies of God, to present your bodies as a living sacrifice, holy and acceptable to God, which is your spiritual worship.*

We bring Him our time and talents, our obedience and surrender, and our gratitude and disappointments.

However, the outer court does not define the fullness of priesthood. Yes, we minister to people the mysteries of the cross in the outer court in many revelatory and practical ways. Yet, after we have finished ministering to people, we should leave the outer court to enter the Holy Place. We turn towards God in the inner court.

In both places, we exercise priestly responsibility. Both have eternal value.

Inner Court

The inner court of the tabernacle was physically enclosed. There was no natural light. Crossing the entrance was like entering into another realm. The inner court was divided in two by a curtain separating the Most Holy place from the Holy Place. Only the priests were allowed into the Holy Place. This space was sparsely furnished: a lamp stand, a table for the showbread, and an incense burner. The ark of the covenant, covered by the mercy seat, was behind the curtain in the Most Holy Place, watched over by two golden cherubim.

Exodus 25:22: *I will meet with you there, and I will talk with you from above the mercy-seat, from between the two cherubs on the ark of the testimony, of all things which I will give you in commandment to the sons of Israel.*

The priests would enter the first part of the room, called the Holy Place. Nobody could easily pop in with a general prayer request. No. In the inner court, only one focus demanded attention: the Lord Himself. The ministry here has a vertical focus. It is always only about God.

The inner court was not labour-intensive, at least not physically. The showbread was changed only once a week. The incense burner burnt day and night, and the lights on the lampstand could never go out. The priests would stand before God, lifting their hearts to Him in songs, psalms and prayers. These they would sing in chants around the hour, with their hearts turned towards the God of Israel.

Ezekiel 44:16: *They shall enter My sanctuary, and they shall come near My table, to minister to Me, and they shall keep My charge.*

A priest knows how to stand before God until God makes Himself known, or even if God does not make Himself known. He stands in awe, in worship, even in silence. He stands and awaits orders. All horizontal and relational concerns fade away in this vertical stance.

Again: in the outer court, we minster to the needs of people. In the Holy Place, we minister to the Lord of heaven and earth.

Tradition teaches us to use the book of Psalms in liturgical outpouring (chapter 12.3) as we minister to the eternal God. The Psalms were inspired by the Holy Spirit in ancient times, and given to us to be prayed unto the Ancient of Days. The Holy Place is not the place for casual words, or individualistic expressions, as it disturbs the seamless symphony of heaven. Here, selfless worshippers tread carefully in eternal ways, bringing their worship to be united with those of previous generations: an ancient and ongoing song to Him who is enthroned, in harmony with choirs and hosts of angels. This is a holy place.

New Testament Responsibility

God never changes His mind throughout the generations, but He changes the ways in which He expresses His mind, to serve each generation differently in history. In the Old Testament, He spoke to people in a material way, a tangible way, which they could understand. The tangible always pointed towards a spiritual reality. In the New Testament, the Holy Spirit is inside us and help us to see things from a higher dimension, from a Spirit level, to perceive God's mind. He has one mind, and we can grow in understanding His complete picture through revelation unfolding throughout all ages.

Therefore, this structure for the ministry of priests continues to be relevant in the New Testament. We continue to serve believers and unbelievers alike in horizontal and relational responsibilities in our communities and nations. This is a command given by God.

Mark 12:31: *The second is like this: You shall love your neighbour as yourself. There is no other commandment greater than these.*

But our primary duty is to minister to our Creator.

Mark 12:29-30: *The first of all the commandments is, 'Hear, O Israel, the Lord our God is one Lord; and you shall love the Lord your God with all your heart, and with all your soul, and with all your mind, and with all your strength.' This is the first commandment.*

If we lose the balance between these two dimensions, our ministry may become ineffective, and easily opposed by demonic powers. This will be a great loss to the Kingdom of God in our generation.

To acquire a priestly lifestyle, we need to learn how to turn our faces and hearts to God, to present our lives as a daily sacrifice unto Him, for one reason only: He is God. And He is worthy. In these post-modern times we need to learn to pray ancient liturgies in everlasting ways.

We have the practical example of the Jewish priesthood in the tabernacle and the temple. But we can also learn from those who have never stopped to minister to God in unbroken, heavenly service – the angels. In most English translations, we find the word 'minister' twice in **Hebrews 1:14**, referring to the ministry of angels:
Are they not all ministering spirits, sent forth to minister for those who shall be heirs of salvation?

Angels are centred around the throne of God in heaven, focussed on Him in His glory and majesty, calling forth to each other in wonder and amazement. In obedience to God, they have always come to earth to serve God's people when sent. But they don't dwell on earth. The angels would complete their God-given assignments in the earthly realm before they return to their places of adoration around His throne, zealous to minister to Him.

In the original Greek, the first word used for 'ministry' in **Hebrews 1:14** is *diakonea*. Angels would minister to mankind according to their particular assignment. In both Testaments we find angels appearing in obedience to God to carry a particular message, or to protect His people. *Diakonea* is the aspect of ministry that has a horizontal focus, to those we love, those God sent across our paths. The flow of *diakonea* is determined by their needs. This forms the root-word for what we know today as deacons – 'those who serve.'

In Greek, the word describing the second use of the word 'ministry' in **Hebrews 1:14** is *liturgia* - 'being ministering spirits.' This word refers to the ministry of the angels before the throne of God, where they continually use the same words in a repetitive way:
Holy, holy, holy is the Lord God Almighty! All glory, honour and power belong to our God! (**Isaiah 6:3**)

In the Holy Place, liturgical prayers do not change. The minister is completely consumed with the majesty of God, lost in the honour to minister to Him who is bright and regal. The Greek word *liturgia* implies repetition. *Liturgia* does not contain streams of personalised prayers and words, intercession for nations, or spiritual warfare. Those belong to the outer court. In the Holy Place eyes are gazing upon the Lord.

Revelation 4:8ᵇ: *Day and night they never cease to say, 'Holy, holy, holy, is the Lord God Almighty, who was and is and is to come!'*

Those who practice the ministry of *liturgia* regularly, know that *liturgia* prepares our own hearts and the surrounding atmosphere for a fresh outpouring of supplication and intercession, even in the Holy Place, but only after *liturgia* has lifted us into a different dimension of faith and union with God's heart and will.

The *liturgia* is the incense burning before His throne. It ascends, and leaves us with nothing but ashes - a humble gratitude and satisfaction in our own hearts. We were created to bring Him admiration from burning hearts.

Angels are not individualistic, nor do they creatively explore a variety of songs, different themes, or diverse styles in worshiping God. Worship in the Holy Place is eternal and everlasting. It is set and established. As priests on earth, we are invited to join this heavenly river of adoration to minister to the King of kings who is a consuming fire, who is unapproachable light, the Ancient of Days, enthroned forever.

Revelation 8:4: *The smoke of the incense, with the prayers of the saints, rose before God from the hand of the angel.*

God wants His own, eternal words to be prayed before Him. God delights in these monotonous, repetitive prayers, prayed from pure hearts alight with love and gratitude.

Psalm 147:11: *The LORD takes pleasure in those who fear Him, in those who hope in His steadfast love.*

Ministry in the inner court on earth unites with the ministry in the heavenly places, and with the worship of those who went before us through the ages. It becomes an ancient and eternal symphony of adulation, where no individual stands out. All is about Him. All is unto Him. And all is united beyond time, filled with pure love. This is holy ground.

A well-known icon from the 4th century depicts St. Anthony, a saint of both the Orthodox and Catholic traditions, preaching. St. Anthony had a great following of disciples who would spend their days and years with him, longing to be taught. The unique feature of this icon is that he is not facing his followers when he teaches, but his face is turned upwards towards heaven, with his disciples sitting behind him, also gazing toward the heavens with the light of revelation shining on their faces. It is as if St. Anthony is bringing his teaching to heaven, an offering of eternal truth unto God, although heaven does not need theological explanation or instruction. But the heart of this saint, as a humble priest, was lifted up to God at all times, turned towards the throne of heaven, and he gave all his life, all his ministry and wisdom, as an offering to God first of all. His disciples were taken up with him in his teaching, receiving the eternal impartation of Life that his words carried. They experienced rivers of Life from heaven directly flowing into their own inner lives and ministries as St. Anthony's *liturgia* was accepted in heaven. His horizontal ministry was overshadowed by his vertical stance before the throne, and his disciples were transformed from glory to glory, bearing fruit in coming generations and ages.

Our ministry is always first unto God. A life of selfless priestly worship will draw men to obedience, to surrender, and to revelation of God in the world. Nowadays, we are captured, even imprisoned by the needs around us: the demands of networking, marketing, the social mutation of each generation, and the next crisis, or our emotional needs. Our priorities are overtaken by the expectations of our followers, often success-driven, defined by statistics and 'feel-good' programs. And we give the left-over crumbs of our time and hearts to God. We only turn to Him when we need help in a serious crisis, or when we prepare our next sermon.

A very sad reality is that our earthly ministries lack the heavenly release we so long for, the mystical work of the Holy Spirit that truly transforms. Rather, we disciple, teach and council young believers for years, only for them to fall away and blame the Church for their pain and disappointment. This can never glorify God! Something is obviously not right.

We cannot blame the world or our followers, if we ourselves don't follow the eternal ways of God, set out for us in all history. *Liturgia* demands priority over *diakonea*, then our ministry on earth will overflow and prosper in a fruitfulness which lasts forever. And yet, *liturgia* is never a way to avoid *diakonea*. We are called to be priest-kings, so that His authority can seal our fruit. To stand on earth and pray as a priest in the heavens is to proclaim the Lordship of Christ on my land in a practical and actual way, day after day, to build His throne in my ministry.

Watchman Nee (1903 – 1972), the Chinese revivalist, said: 'The thing I fear most is that many of you will go out and win sinners to the Lord and build up believers, without ministering to the Lord Himself. Much so-called service for Him is simply following our natural inclinations. We have such active dispositions that we cannot bear to stay at home, so we run around for our own relief. We may appear to be serving sinners, or serving believers, but all the while we are serving our own flesh.'[79]

The priest is to bring God worship and adoration, to draw near God and stand before Him.

Ezekiel 44:15: *But the priests, the Levites...shall come near Me to minister to Me, and they shall stand before Me to offer to Me the fat and the blood, says the Lord God.*

---

79.   *www.sermonindex.net/modules/articles/index.php?view=article&aid=6923*

Watchman Nee continues: 'To come into the presence of God and kneel before Him for an hour demands all the strength we possess. We have to be violent to hold that ground.'

Entering the Holy Place

While doing the physical work in the outer court, priests were dressed in suitable clothing for practical word. This 'normal' clothing represents humanity. The priest identifies with the normal man-on-the-street in their sickness, weakness to sin and social responsibilities. Priests do not minister from a spiritually superior position with presumed holiness.

Hebrews 5:1,2: *For every high priest taken from among men is ordained for men in the things pertaining to God, so that he may offer both gifts and sacrifices for sins, who can have compassion on the ignorant and on those who are out of the way. For he himself also is compassed with weakness.*

Whilst in the outer court with crowds of people, priests are dressed in servanthood and brokenness, remembering his own fallenness. When we attend to the painful needs of society, we are deeply aware that we could suffer in similar ways. This is very important.

Work in the outer court was laborious, and none of this sweaty residue could enter into His Holy Place. If we minister in true humility to humanity, some of the dust from the outer court will settle on us, in our thoughts and emotions. This includes those we minister to, their mortality, anxiety and pain, or the injustice and hopelessness they suffer. In close contact of heart and spirit we are affected by the stories and events of each day. At the end of a counselling session, we need to lay down the burdens and details so that it does not continue to affect and burden us in prayer, nor influence the next conversation we may have. Leaders carry detailed knowledge of their flock, their finances and marriages, their confessions and struggles, and we need time to lay it all down to meet with God in a fresh way in worship. In true priestly work, a transfer from sheep to shepherd does take place. The weight of hopelessness is shifted from those who come for prayer ministry, and although Jesus truly carries our pain and injustice as the Great High Priest, the reality is that the priest experiences the pain and weight for a period of time. At the end of a long day, the exhaustion and 'dirt' of the outer court activities settled upon us. We cannot enter the inner court in such a way.

Ezekiel 44:18: *They shall not bind themselves with anything that causes sweat.*

Sweat is a sign of the curse of mankind after the Fall, to work the land in our own strength, outside the grace and fullness of God's presence.[80] When the blessing of God is absent in our lives and ministries, fleshly effort becomes necessary in trying to be effective. Planning, strategizing, exhorting, urging, striving, labouring, reconciling, and fundraising, even fasting and prayer cause us to sweat. Sweat cannot be taken into the Holy Place. All earthly realities and stress need to be washed away before entering the Holy Place to minister to God. It calls for discipline to surrender thoughts and feelings, all knowledge and facts, expertise, burdens etc. The mind and emotions are washed and restored to innocent peace. I leave behind the outer court.

Then I am dressed in fresh, clean linen, to enter the inner court.

Ezekiel 44:16-18: *[The priests] shall enter My sanctuary, and they shall approach My table, to minister to Me, and they shall*

---

80.   Genesis 3:19

keep My charge. When they enter the gates of the inner court, they shall wear linen garments. They shall have nothing of wool on them, while they minister at the gates of the inner court, and within. They shall have linen turbans on their heads, and linen undergarments around their waists. They shall not bind themselves with anything that causes sweat.

The priest goes through ritual washing to dress freshly: our shortcomings are covered. We shake off our own weaknesses and fallenness. The dust, sweat and memories are washed away. Our humanity is not just covered, but all pain and sin is absorbed in the Lamb that was slain, our own imperfections bedecked with His grace. As we enter into the inner court we are focussed, even consumed, with His dwelling presence only. We are here to minister to God.

In the New Testament those who believed in the Son of God, are clothed in Christ.[81] Therefore we are able to enter the Holy Place, approaching the throne of grace.

Galatians 3:27 (NASB): *For all who were baptized into Christ have clothed yourselves with Christ.*

As the Holy Spirit rests upon us in the Holy Place, we minister in power and glory in the secret place, alongside heavenly hosts.

Worship is structured through wisdom. If we lack understanding of the different clothing codes in the outer and inner court, we may leave the Holy Place after an heavenly encounter, and speak down to people in the outer court as if they are the weak ones, the bad ones, and we are the supra-spiritual ones. Be careful. Fear God. This does not glorify God, neither can it bear fruit.

---

81.   Isaiah 61:10

All spiritual work, both in the outer and inner court, is done in obedience, to please God. None is better than the other, and none is inferior to the other. It is vital to understand that we cannot choose which one we prefer. It is our responsibility to maintain both the inner court ministry unto God, as well as the outer court ministry to society. Our ministry in the Holy Place unto God urges us outward to a world needing salvation.

Priestly garments

Exodus 28:2-3 (MKJV): *You shall make holy garments for Aaron your brother, for glory and for beauty. And you shall speak to all the wise-hearted, whom I have filled with the spirit of wisdom, that they make Aaron's garments to consecrate him, so that he may minister to Me in the priest's office.*

Priestly garments were designed by God, and fashioned by those who were 'wise-hearted, filled with the spirit of wisdom.' Every small detail was symbolic and prophetic, with an undeniable purpose: the minister to God!

Exodus 28:4: *These are the garments which they shall make: a breastplate, an ephod, a robe, a skillfully woven tunic, a turban, and a sash. So they shall make holy garments for Aaron your brother and his sons, that he may minister to Me as priest.*

These clothes were worn by nobody else but the priests. It was holy unto the Lord, and set the priests apart from the rest of Israel.

Priestly Breastplate

The names of the twelve tribes were engraved on the breastplate.

Exodus 28:15-21,29: *You shall make the breast-piece of judgment with embroidered work. After the work of the ephod you shall make it; of gold, blue, and purple, and scarlet, and fine twined bleached linen, you shall make it. It shall be square, doubled; a span the length of it, and a span the breadth of it. You shall set in it settings of stones, four rows of stones. The first row shall be a ruby, topaz, and carbuncle in the row. And the second row: an emerald, a sapphire. and a diamond. And the third row: a jacinth, an agate, and an amethyst. And the fourth row: a chrysolite, and an onyx, and a jasper. They shall be set in gold in their fillings. And the stones shall be with the names of the sons of Israel, twelve, according to their names, like the engravings of a signet. They shall be each one with his name according to the twelve tribes. Aaron shall bear the names of the sons of Israel in the breast-piece of judgment upon his heart, when he goes in to the holy place, for a memorial before the LORD continually.*

The high priest was responsible before God to intercede for all twelve tribes of Israel, to hear their confessions, their problems, and brought them teaching and understanding. He would receive their sacrifices and offerings, and present them before the Lord. Whenever Aaron entered before God on behalf of His people into the Holy Place, he did not mention the tribes one by one, neither did he discuss the long lists of problems with God as we nowadays do in intercession. Aaron never presented to God options on how He should solve these numerous issues. Or even worse, Aaron never demanded any particular response from God.

According to **Leviticus chapter 16**, the high priest went through ceremonial preparation on the Day of Atonement to enter the Holy Place. After the sacrifices and rituals were completed, he would put on His priestly garments. This detailed, mystical sacrament brought him to identify entirely with Israel, with the joys and the struggles of the nation as a whole. He was not separate from his people.

He was not interceding from a distance. He was not just carrying their names on his clothes. He became one with the people of God. He carried them within his inner being into the Holy Place, to present them to God from his heart.

The priest was in complete harmony with God's heart. When he eventually put on the breastplate, he would already be one in spirit with God, as God shares the priest's pain for the people: 'What is in your heart for them is just an echo of what is on My heart. I am receiving all your burdens and requests for the twelve tribes. Go in peace.' Thus, Aaron could surrender all the burdens to God, and could go outside to bless the nation in the Name of the God of Abraham, Isaac and Jacob, their covenant God.[82]

Consequently, a complete release went forth to each family, to all of society, to shepherds, fisherman and soldiers alike, including women and children. The blessing was instituted to enable the nation of Israel to prosper, and to worship with fresh revelation. What a responsibility for the priest to stand between God's chosen people and the Holy One Himself, to release health and prosperity for another day, wisdom and insight for another year, whilst the breastplate was resting closely on his heart.

In the new dispensation after the cross, we no longer enter the physical temple in Jerusalem. We enter our inner hearts where He dwells through His Spirit. Within our hearts, we approach the throne of God. We humbly carry in our hearts the responsibility assigned to us from heaven, asking for a gracious touch for those we are responsible for.

Imagine the Church in any generation being true priests, being in tune with God in the Holy Place, having one heart

---

82.   Numbers 6:22-27

and will with God. What a heavenly release and impact would be released upon earth, to the people entrusted to us!

Jesus Christ, our everlasting High Priest, continues to carry all people in His humanity before the altar in heaven,[83] interceding continuously for our complete transformation.

Hebrews 7:25: *Therefore He is able also to save to the uttermost those who come unto God by Him, since He ever lives to make intercession for them.*

We are engraved on His palms with the nails of the cross.[84]

Turban

Exodus 28:36-38: *You shall make a plate of pure gold and engrave on it, like the engraving of a signet, 'Holy to the LORD.' And you shall fasten it on the turban by a cord of blue. It shall be on the front of the turban. It shall be on Aaron's forehead, and Aaron shall bear any guilt from the holy things that the people of Israel consecrate as their holy gifts. It shall regularly be on his forehead, that they may be accepted before the LORD.*

The turban and gold plate tied to the forehead of the high priest proclaimed his consecration to God: Holy unto the Lord!

In **Zechariah chapter 3**, Israel returned from Babylon, and we find Joshua, the priest clothed in filthy clothes. It is unthinkable for a priest to be identified with unrighteous behaviour. Even more indicative, the priest had lost his turban, as he no longer lived as consecrated unto God.

---

83. Revelation 6:9; 8:3,5
84. Isaiah 49:6

Whilst in exile, it is clear that they did not keep themselves separate from the surrounding nations. They became ordinary, doing life as the Gentiles did. Israel and the priesthood were no longer set apart unto God. They fitted into Babylonian society.

As we continue reading Zechariah chapter three, we see the longsuffering of God forgiving the high-priest, and clothing him anew:

Zechariah 3:4-5: *The angel said to those who were standing before Him, 'Remove the filthy garments from him.' And to him he said, 'Behold, I have taken your iniquity away from you, and I will clothe you with pure vestments.' And I said, 'Let them put a clean turban on his head.' So they put a clean turban on his head and clothed him with garments.*

Priests should never fit in. Priests are holy unto God. Priests without a turban is shamed before heaven.

Furniture in the Holy Place

1Corinthians 3:16: *Do you not know that you are God's temple and that God's Spirit dwells in you?*

Our bodies are temples unto God. To increase His dwelling Presence on earth,[85] we should furnish the inner chambers of our heart with the furniture of the temple.

---

85. Ephesians 3:17

Altar of Incense

How appropriate to call this piece of furniture an 'altar.' This was not merely a censor in which incense was burnt, but it was an altar where an offering of praise was brought to burn day and night.

Hebrews 13:15: *Through Him then let us continually offer up a sacrifice of praise to God, that is, the fruit of lips that acknowledge His Name.*

The recipe for the incense used in the Holy Place was prescribed in precision, each ingredient carrying deep prophetic implications.

Exodus 30:34-38: *The LORD said to Moses, Take to yourself sweet spices, galbanum, and onycha, and galbanum; sweet spices with pure frankincense, a part of each one. You shall make it a perfume, an incense according to the art of the perfumer, salted, pure and holy. And you shall beat some of it very small, and put it before the testimony in the tabernacle of the congregation, where I will meet with you. It shall be most holy to you. And the perfume which you shall make, you shall not make any for yourselves according to the way it is made. It shall be holy to you for LORD. Whoever shall make any like that, to smell of it, shall even be cut off from his people.*

Incense refers to our lives of prayer, our liturgical ministry brought before Him, while the fire is the fellowship with the Holy Spirit. The incense to be burnt in the Holy Place is described as sweet, perfumed, salted, pure and holy. We cannot offer bitter prayers to God. We cannot bring a bland, or foul offering to Him. Salt protects us from the rotting influences of the world. Purity and holiness are the only acceptable incense we can offer to our King and

Bridegroom. This makes our prayers innocent, acceptable and powerfully effective.

Revelation 5:8: *When He had taken the book, the four living creatures and the twenty-four elders fell down before the Lamb, each one having harps and golden vials full of incense, which are the prayers of the saints.*

According to the writings of the early centuries, these twenty-four elders refer to a particular group of angels called Angelic Priests. They have a distinct ministry to receive our liturgical prayers in golden bowls, adding their own prayers to it, and present it to God on the throne. Once these bowls are filled, in God's perfect timing, He tips the bowls and we see momentous results in the heavens and on earth.

Revelation 8:3-5: *Another angel came and stood at the altar, having a golden censer. And much incense was given to him, so that he should offer it with the prayers of all saints on the golden altar before the throne. And the smoke of the incense which came with the prayers of the saints, ascended up before God from the angel's hand. The angel took the censer and filled it with fire from the altar, and cast it into the earth. Voices and thunderings and lightnings and an earthquake occurred.*

This angelic priest is working with mankind in things related to the Kingdom of God on earth. Such liturgical intercession bears everlasting fruit, beyond limits. 'Voices' are divine signals to escape judgment, warning sounds in the nations and the body of Christ to call us to return to righteousness. 'Thunderings' is another level of warning, even terror, that alerts the hearts that are sleeping and did not obey the 'voices.' 'Lightnings' is a light guiding us towards repentance and obeying the ways and truth of God. An 'earthquake' is a tremor that wakes up all, changing the status quo.

In our days, many people depend on prayer meetings for prayer. When alone at home, our incense is weak, interrupted, most days non existing. Corporate prayer meetings energise us, and we are released, encouraged and built up in the spirit. Corporate prayer has an important place in society. However, it is of absolute importance that each person brings their own incense before the Lord in the secret place.[86] We cannot carry the corporate priestly function in our nations until we have learnt the discipline to minister to God in private. God longs for incense each day.

We need an Incense Altar in our inner temple, lit and burning with sweet fragrant *liturgia*. This is our first responsibility as priest-kings, just as Jesus, our High Priest, brings His incense to the Father.

Mark 1:35 *Rising very early in the morning, while it was still dark, He departed and went out to a desolate place, and there He prayed.*

Lampstand

Exodus 25:31,32: *You shall also make a lampstand of pure gold; the lampstand shall be of hammered work. Its shaft, its branches, its bowls, its ornamental knobs, and flowers shall be of one piece. And six branches shall come out of its sides: three branches of the lampstand out of one side, and three branches of the lampstand out of the other side.*

The light of the lampstand refers to the Holy Spirit.

Revelation 4:5[b]: *Seven lamps of fire were burning before the throne, which are the seven Spirits of God.*

---

86.   Matthew 6:6

The seven Spirits of God indicate that He is a mystical Person with numerous facets and aspects, with countless depths and dimensions. The light of the lampstand was given to us to grow in knowledge and insight, even of the Trinity.

As a priest takes his stand in the inner court, his own inner life is mystically enlightened, to recognise his own crookedness and darkness first, but also to see God's goodness and glory, His ways and wisdom, His eternal mysteries. This grace prepares the priest to draw near to God, into deeper union with God.

As we stand in His light, filled with knowledge and insight, our ministry to Him births prophetic clarity on earth, and the world outside will be enlightened and awakened to turn to God.

Why is the world so dark? Satan rules in darkness,[87] and wants darkness to prevail. The god of this world works against any life-giving light,[88] to obscure the minds of people and nations. This darkness is not a natural darkness, the absence of light. Rather, it actively rejects light. Darkness is a power at work.[89] It requires the power of redemption to push back our present darkness.

Our generation is unable to hear the Gospel, to receive it by faith in our hearts. Darkness covers our minds, and we are incapacitated to respond to the Good News of Jesus Christ.

2Corinthians 4:4: *The god of this world has blinded the minds of the unbelieving ones, so that the light of the glorious gospel of Christ (who is the image of God) should not dawn on them.*

---

87. Ephesians 6:12
88. John 1:4
89. **Luke 22:53:** *But this is your hour, and the power of darkness.*

Priests know how to light the lamps in our inner court, to push away the darkness from the minds of people, to prepare the way for salvation and truth to be received in society, before we go into the outer court to minister to the lost. Priests in the heavenly places free the minds of a generation to receive divine light, to turn to God in repentance.

Priests who are disciplined, focussed and trained in the secret place will bear divine light to the world.

John 12:36: *While you have the Light, believe in the Light so that you may become sons of Light.*

This is a mystical work of prayer, with immeasurable fruit. The enemy would rather keep us busy, striving for success and recognition in the outer court. He distracts us from focussed work in the inner court. Without His light shining within our inner darkness, into the confusion and misunderstandings, into questions and unanswered prayer, we can easily be lead astray.

Sadly, the increasing and thickening of darkness in our generation is not only the activity of the evil one, but also due to the absence of priestly worship in the Church. Indeed, ministry to God in the secret place has the power to break the power of darkness in our generation.

Table of Showbread

This table was made of acacia wood and overlaid with pure gold. It stood on the right side of the Holy Place across from the lampstand, with the altar of incense between them. The showbread consisted of twelve unleavened loaves representing the tribes of Israel. Placing these breads weekly on the table in God's presence symbolized the consecration of Israel unto the Lord, and their acceptance of God to be their God.

Exodus 25:30: *You shall set upon the table Bread of the Presence before Me always.*

It was the responsibility of the priest on duty to bake the bread with fine flour. Each Sabbath, the priests would put fresh bread on the table. Incense was burnt on top of these loaves, day and night, to consecrate this offering – the twelve tribes - unto God.

'Showbread' was also called 'bread of the presence' or 'bread of the face(s)', as it was always in the Lord's presence. His face was always turned towards, and shining upon Israel with favour. God desires to have close communion with His people. The Table of Showbread is an invitation to fellowship, to share a meal. God longs for mankind to be satisfied and fulfilled in Him, and this invitation is always open.

Christ is the showbread, who came to earth from heaven as the 'Bread of Life' to give eternal life to all who would partake of Him. He was broken on the cross, and was distributed to all for deep inner satisfaction of our emptiness and endless longing for forgiveness, and belonging.

John 6:35: *I am the bread of life. He who comes to Me shall never hunger, and he who believes on Me shall never thirst.*[90]

Priests should regularly change the bread which is placed on the table of our inner hearts. Our fellowship with God is always to be fresh, having a special power to attract

---

90.   John 6:50-51

others, a flavour. When somebody asks for bread - advice, prayer, or ministry of any kind - we cannot afford to give tasteless, hardened bread. In this case, their hearts will not be touched. Our ministries should be nourishing and satisfying so that our followers lack nothing, and will not seek to gratify the flesh in worldly ways. Instead, they will turn to have communion with Him who was broken for us.

From the Divine Liturgy of John Chrysostom (347-407AD)

For Thou art the Offeror and the Offered,
the Receiver and the Received, O Christ our God,
and to Thee we ascribe glory, together with
Thy Father, who is from everlasting,
and Thine all-holy, good, and life-creating Spirit,
now and ever, and unto ages of ages.

Priest-Kings in
the Old Testament

You shall be my people, and I will be your God.

Jeremiah 30:22

As we discover the divine structure given to us in the Garden of Eden, the greatness of the office of being Priest-Kings may initially seem far-fetched, or supra-spiritual. And yet, if these are truly eternal realities, then we should find tangible examples in past centuries of those who walked in these eternal ways.

Old Testament Examples

God revealed His purposes through the lives of people who served and feared Him.

Patriarch Abraham

After the Flood, evil and corruption continued to prevail on earth. However, God's purposes for mankind remained unchangeable. He did not succumb to disappointment or frustration with mankind. God continued steadfastly to prepare redemption for all mankind, to restore His Kingdom on earth. God searched for a man to draw near to Him, and He found this person in Abraham:

James 2:23: *Abraham believed God, and it was counted to him as righteousness – and he was called a friend of God.*

God blessed Abraham exactly as He blessed Adam in **Genesis 1:28**, and Abraham became a ruler on the earth. He was even granted the same promises as Adam. How did this practically unfold in his life?

Abraham sojourned in a tent. Wherever Abraham journeyed, he would pitch his tent, and build an altar.[91]

---

91.   Genesis 12:7,8; 13:18

The altar is a testimony of Abraham's continuous fellowship with God. Abraham was a priest unto God. The tent symbolises temporary accommodation, a sojourner on earth *en route* to a permanent, heavenly city.[92] Abraham did not find security in a permanent dwelling. He was free from material and earthly realities that could hold him down; free to obey and follow God wherever and whenever He called, even although he was a very rich man.

Abraham's tent was not merely a physical tent for accommodation and shade, it became a dwelling place of God, journeying onwards towards an eternal, heavenly goal. The presence of God, due to the unfailing worship on the altar, transformed and consecrated this normal family tent into a divine tent, a Tent of Fellowship,[93] a prophetic pre-tabernacle sanctuary.

The presence of God in the tent was the heart of Abraham's identity, as he remained to be a newcomer in the land of the Canaanites, a tent-dweller who owned no land. He was an outsider, a nomad.

We recognise Abraham's authority in the victories in all the battles he fought. He fought external battles with visible enemies, the kings of the lands promised to him and his descendants. He also fought to restore Lot, his cousin, and was victorious in these physical encounters.[94] However, he also had to fight invisible enemies, opposing demonic realities. When God intended to cut the covenant with Abraham, it was demonically opposed.[95] In this covenant, distinct promises about the restoration of the

---

92. Hebrews 11:10
93. Genesis 18
94. Genesis 14
95. Genesis 15:11

inheritance of the land (the earth) to God's chosen people, was proclaimed. Abraham battled an invisible war with vultures, symbolic of opposing evil spirits, until sunset. He triumphed and was granted the promises which involved future generations – both for the Jews, and for all nations.

Abraham also fought internal battles of faith:

Genesis 15:2: *Abram said, 'Lord God, what will You give me, since I am going childless, and the steward of my house is this Eliezer of Damascus?'*

Genesis chapter fifteen gives us insight in a very low stage in Abraham's life. He was tempted with doubt, to give up, to question God. Internal battles are difficult ones to endure and conquer. And yet, we know that Abraham did not just conquer his insecurities and reservations, but he became the father of faith, who obeyed God even in being willing to sacrifice his own son promised by God almost thirty years earlier, the son he awaited for so long.

Hebrews 11:17-19: *By faith Abraham, when he was tested, offered up Isaac, and he who had received the promises was in the act of offering up his only son, of whom it was said, 'Through Isaac shall your offspring be named.' He considered that God was able even to raise him from the dead, from which, figuratively speaking, he did receive him back.*

His inner victories humble us in our pursuit of following after, and trusting God. He overcame impatience and unbelief. He became the father of faith for all generations.

Years later, in **Genesis chapter twenty-three**, we find that Sarai died. Abraham negotiated to buy a piece of land as a burial site for his wife. The inhabitants of the land (the sons of Heth) wanted to give the land to Abraham in respect of him. They acknowledged Abraham's authority by calling him *a mighty prince among us*.[96] They saw him as a ruler, and they welcomed his authority and wisdom. We don't read of any fear or distrust. They loved his presence among them as he brought about peace, prosperity and stability to the nations where he sojourned.

Forgive me for underlining these weighty principles in Abraham's life: his every-day tent became a spiritual space for the Eternal God to dwell with Him on earth amongst the heathen nations. His altar opened up the vertical dimension which established his authority, which was not imposed on the foreign nations, but rather it was recognised and welcomed. As the Gentiles acknowledged Abraham as *a mighty prince* in Canaan, it is clear that God's authority was released on earth through this humble man.

Abraham's life is sharply contrasted with Lot's, his cousin. Lot also knew the Lord, but we don't read about structured worship in his life. Lot also lived in tents, but they were mere earthly shelters. Lot lacked an altar at the core of his days. It is clear that Lot had no spiritual or relational authority to exercise in Sodom and Gomorrah – even his sons-in-law laughed at him.[97] He had no righteous impact or influence in these godless cities, no fruit. Lot did experience grace and salvation when Sodom and Gomorrah were judged, but only due to the intercession of his uncle Abraham.[98]

Moses – Shepherd and Father

The authority of Abraham manifested as an individual, within one family. However, God's intentions were to rule

---

96. Genesis 23:6
97. Genesis 19:14
98. Genesis 18 and 19

in and through nations on earth. In the life of Moses, we see God's dealing with one chosen nation – a nation born from Abraham's descendants.

Once God led the Israelites out of Egypt, having crossed the Red Sea, God made His intentions immediately clear. He revealed His eternal purposes to this new-born nation, laying a foundation to build an everlasting Kingdom of God on earth. In **Exodus chapter 19**, God called Moses up the mountain to share His heart and objectives, and commanded Moses to build a sanctuary for Him amidst His people.

Exodus 25:8: *Let them make Me a sanctuary, so that I may dwell among them.*

God was leading the Israelites towards the Promised Land, but there was more in His heart than a geographical journey from Egypt to Canaan. He wanted to lay foundations for future generations, to reveal eternal intentions in His heart. God's desire to dwell among His people, as in the Garden of Eden, was evident. God did not want to speak to His people through a mediator, Moses, from a distant, fiery mountain. He gave detailed instructions on how to prepare a place where He could dwell in the heart of the camp, right in their midst as a divine Neighbour. He wanted to establish His throne in their midst, as a testimony to the surrounding nations of His kingdom, as a foretaste of eternity. God also gave Moses the Ten Commandments: demarcations of Love. Each commandment points to righteousness and neighbourly love, for Israel to honour their King, and bring hope and life to all nations.

Exodus 19:4-6: *You have seen what I did to the Egyptians, and I bore you on eagles' wings and brought you to Myself. And now if you will obey My voice indeed, and keep My covenant, then you* *shall be a peculiar treasure to Me above all the nations; for all the earth is Mine. And you shall be to Me a kingdom of priests and a holy nation.*

Israel became a blue-print for other nations to gain understanding of God's eternal ways. God did not favour the Israelites over the other nations, but rather His intention was to extend His Kingdom to all nations through the Jews.

Verse 4 states, *I brought you to myself.* God longs for restored fellowship with His creatures, for worship, so that we can receive much needed healing and restoration in our stance before Him. In **verse 5** we find the conditions for His people: *If you will indeed obey My voice and keep My covenant you shall be a treasured possession among all people…you shall be to Me a Kingdom of Priests and a Holy Nation.*

Israel was chosen to become a kingdom of priests with vibrant and pure worship, intercessors with authority for the nations, a channel through which His life could flow to earth, to prepare the nations for His Everlasting Reign.

These were the basic guidelines given to Moses:

† Build an altar for daily sacrifices
† A tent, dedicated to God
† Obedience to all the commandments
† Then God will dwell in their midst
† The nations will know and recognise God as the Most High God

We recognise all these principles in the life of Abraham, about 500 years prior to Moses. How did all of this come about?

The Firstborn of Israel

As the Israelites applied the blood of the Passover lamb to the doorposts of their houses, the angel of death passed over the Jews, and only the firstborn of the Egyptians were killed. The firstborn of Israel were saved only in God's mercy, and because of their obedience to His commandments.[99] It was God's intention to set apart unto Himself the firstborn of each Jewish family as His chosen priests who would enter into the sanctuary to stand before Him, to minister at His altar, and to intercede for His people. God made provision for every family to minister to Him in the Holy Place. God always includes all. He never favours one over another.[100]

Sadly, Israel did not treasure this generous invitation to be a Kingdom of Priests unto God. In the unfortunate story of **Exodus chapter 32**, as Moses delayed coming down the mountain, they asked Aaron to make for them a god to go before them. On the mountain, God was preparing Moses at that very moment to build a sanctuary for Him in their midst, for God to be near His people. But the nation's insecurity and lukewarm love towards God led to the creation of a substitute Golden Calf. As Moses came down the mountain, distraught with pain due to their rejection of God, the tribe of Levi came to his side with swords and killed three thousand of their brothers.[101] What a tremendously sad day!

Once again, the ways of God were frustrated by the hard-heartedness of man. The outcome of this sad chapter in history was that the Levites were set aside as the only tribe

---

99. Exodus 13:1-2; Numbers 18:15
100. Romans 2:11
101. Exodus 32:26-28

who could serve Him in His tabernacle, rather than all the firstborn in Israel.

Numbers 3:11-13: *The LORD spoke to Moses, saying, 'Behold, I have taken the Levites from among the people of Israel instead of every firstborn who opens the womb among the people of Israel. The Levites shall be Mine, for all the firstborn are mine. On the day that I struck down all the firstborn in the land of Egypt, I consecrated for My own all the firstborn in Israel, both of man and of beast. They shall be Mine: I am the LORD.'*

These are indications of how the fullness of God's authority on earth is directly linked to the worship and obedience of His people. Our actions frustrate His plans again and again, and limit the manifestation of His Kingdom among the nations.

Inauguration of the Tabernacle

Exodus chapter 40 underlines for us the fruit of complete obedience to God's instructions.

Exodus 40:16: *This Moses did; according to all that the LORD commanded him, so he did.*

Once Moses and the Israelites obeyed each and every detailed instruction of God concerning the construction of the Altar and the Tent of Meeting, a divine cloud covered the tent, and the glory of the Lord filled the tabernacle. His presence came to dwell among His people, visible in the fiery column at night, and the cloud covering them during the hot, desert days. Whenever the cloud lifted, the people would pack up to follow their God.

In the tabernacle, right in the midst of Israel, certain aspects of Eden were restored. God was no longer far away and distant. He was 'walking again' with mankind on earth. His presence was for their protection and guidance, and the neighbouring nations discovered the God of Israel, acknowledging that He was greater than their own gods. For forty years in the wilderness, the Israelites never lost a battle, although they were not trained soldiers. A divine authority fought on their behalf.

God's presence was their home and safety, their provision of water and food, the source of health (unless they rebelled and complained) and, consequently, a general well-being of *shalom* radiated from them. He was their God, and they were His people.[102] They were different from all nations on earth, a heavenly nation, proclaiming His character to all.

The Israelites knew and understood these eternal principles. The Law was constantly read and taught in their families. When they followed His instructions in obedience, His authority was like a banner of love over them, filling the heathen nations with jealousy and fear. A nation walking in His ways, extending His Kingdom on earth, was a step forward in history to prepare all nations for His eternal rulership.

Samuel, Prophet and Priest

Samuel had an established vertical focus. Although it was his mother Hannah who initially dedicated him unto the Lord, he was single-minded in his service and love for God. Multiple times he is described in this priestly stance.[103]

---

102.   Exodus 29:45; Leviticus 26:45
103.   1Samuel 2:11b,21,26

1Samuel 3:1ᵃ: *Now the boy Samuel was ministering to the LORD in the presence of Eli.*

Samuel grew up in an atmosphere of corrupted priesthood. Eli was the high priest, although not heeding the warning of God to his household.[104] Eli's sons Hophni and Phinehas were described as *worthless* – sons of Belial.[105] Eli's heart was desensitised and hardened through excess and ease. Therefore God's favour and authority was absent from Israel. In a battle against the Philistines, Israel lost the Ark of the Covenant, Hophni and Phinehas were both killed, as well as thousands of other soldiers. Eli died after receiving this news from the battlefield. Ichabod was born,[106] as God's glory lifted from the nation. Israel was no longer a nation of priest-kings, but a nation subdued as servants by Gentile nations.

Samuel was not hardened by this godless behaviour surrounding him. He remained focussed and pure in his ministry to God. His God-fearing, vertical stance held him secure, and eventually his righteous authority was recognised throughout Israel,[107] in becoming the nation's spiritual leader. He confronted idolatry,[108] restored the Word of the Lord to its rightful place in Israel,[109] and led the nation in true worship.[110]

The authority of his inner life in the heavenly realm manifested on earth in a mystical way in his victory against the Philistines.[111] The cities which the Philistines had taken

---

104.   1Samuel 2:27-36
105.   1Samuel 2:12-17
106.   1Samuel 4:19-11
107.   1Samuel 3:20
108.   1Samuel 7:3-4
109.   1Samuel 3:19,21
110.   1Samuel 7:17ᵇ
111.   1Samuel 7:5-12

from Israel were restored. Moreover, there was peace between Israel and the Amorites.

As a true priest, he 'ruled' in Israel. The secret of his life is summarised in **1Samuel 7:13:** *The hand of the Lord was against the Philistines all the days of Samuel.*

One man's dedication to God established victory and peace for the whole nation of Israel, until the day of his death. He withstood in the spirit the enemies, both physical and spiritual, and channelled the authority of God on earth.

We often blame politicians and terrorists for the unrest in our societies. Psychologists and sociologists analyse domestic violence and gangster culture to advise governments on how to restore calm to our cities. Is it possible that the lack of priestly worship in the lives of Christians may contribute to the lack of peace on our streets?

Daniel in Exile

Daniel's childhood was violently disrupted when he was taken to Babylon as a captive. He was made a eunuch, and lived as an exile in a foreign land under military sovereignty and much idolatry. We know little of Daniel's parents, but it is clear that they laid a foundation within their young son. Daniel refused to walk in the ways of the Babylonians. He took a risk in refusing to eat food sacrificed to idols so as to prevent himself from being defiled.[112]

Even in adverse circumstances, Daniel remained single-mindedly focussed on ministering to God. He bowed in his daily routine in opening his window towards Jerusalem,

---

112.   Daniel 1:8-9

the resting place of God, in prayer unto God for his people. His heart was set on obedience to God at all cost. Even when faced with humiliation and persecution, he remained steadfast, never neglecting his vertical, priestly stance before God.

Daniel 6:10: *When Daniel knew that the document had been signed, he went to his house where he had windows in his upper chamber open toward Jerusalem. He got down on his knees three times a day and prayed and gave thanks before his God, as he had done previously.*

In his lifetime Daniel served under three pagan kings in Babylon. All three of these mighty kings acknowledged the authority of Daniel, and the supremacy of the God of Daniel.

Daniel 2:46-48: *Then King Nebuchadnezzar fell on his face, prostrate before Daniel, and commanded that they should present an offering and incense to him. The king answered Daniel, and said, 'Truly your God is the God of gods, the Lord of kings, and a revealer of secrets, since you could reveal this secret.'*

Daniel 5:29: *Then Belshazzar gave the command, and Daniel was clothed with purple, a chain of gold was put around his neck, and a proclamation was made about him, that he should be the third ruler in the kingdom.*

Daniel 6:25-27: *Then King Darius wrote: 'To all peoples, nations, and languages that dwell in all the earth: Peace be multiplied to you. I make a decree that in every dominion of my kingdom men must tremble and fear before the God of Daniel. For He is the living God, and steadfast forever; His kingdom is the one which shall not be destroyed, and His dominion shall endure to the end. He delivers and rescues, and He works signs and wonders in heaven and on earth, who has delivered Daniel from the power of the lions.'*

Daniel's temporary 'tent' was a simple, open window looking towards Jerusalem. His 'altar' was his tears and humble repentance for the sins of his nation, three times every day, faithfully. God was revealed and glorified in Babylon, and the great Nebuchadnezzar, himself considered to be a god, even bowed before the God of Israel.[113]

God's Kingdom manifested in Babylon through an eunuch in exile, a true priest-king.

Those who Rejected God's Eternal Ways

We will look at the lives of Samson and king Saul, both preceding the rulership of David, but sharply contrasting David's life in their rejection of God's eternal principles.

Samson - the Nazirite

The first mention of the nation of Philistines we find in the book of Joshua. Although Joshua successfully conquered many kings,[114] in **Joshua chapter 13** we read that there were still large territories within the Promised Land possessed by Canaanite nations. In v. 2, the Philistines are mentioned: *This is the land that yet remains: all the regions of the Philistines.* There is a chilling truth hidden in this single verse. Under Joshua's leadership, Israel settled within the boundaries of their promised destiny, yet they never conquered the Philistines. Is it acceptable to co-exist with the enemy who is destined for destruction? Can we peacefully settle next to the enemies of our spirit?

113.　Daniel 2:46
114.　Joshua 12:7-23

The Philistines used to be the main occupiers of the Promised Land. Allegorically, they can be typified as the 'Self,' the fallen nature which often dominates our lives, despite having been bought by Christ in His redemption. The Philistines represents every aspect in me where I, me and myself are justified, excused, exalted, uncrucified and alive. Wherever the Philistines reign, Christ and the cross have little authority. It represents the areas of my life which resists being confronted; not reflecting the crucified and resurrected Jesus in relationships, finances, thoughts and emotions, in my marriage, family and ministry. Too much inner territory is ruled over by the Philistines.

The Philistines are again mentioned when an angel appears to a barren woman in a field to announce the birth of Samson *'who will begin to save Israel from the hand of the Philistines.'*[115] Samson's calling was clearly pronounced before his birth. God always provides everything we need to fulfil His calling in our lives. And yet, our calling needs to mature within us before it can manifest and bear fruit externally. It goes without saying that we cannot separate our outer battles in our calling, with our personal battles in our inner lives. The one is the preparation for the full manifestation of the other. Once we are victorious in our inner battles, it can lead to victory in our family and ministry, all through grace.

God is always faithful, and He gave Samson the ability and grace to walk in victory over his inner enemies of the ego and passions. God would have trained and prepared him in every inner aspect to conquer the external enemies, the Philistines.

---

115. Judges 13:5

For a time Samson dealt supernaturally with the Philistines, killing even thousands,[116] and God's justice manifested through him. Yet, in his personal life, Samson's ego was prominent, even dominant. He was a powerful man, strong in the flesh. He considered the grace granted to him lightly, played with sin and sinners until the Philistines trapped him through deception. Immediately the presence of God lifted from him.[117] He became weak like any other. He became an ordinary man, clearly not set apart unto God.

The very people Samson was called and anointed to destroy at his birth,[118] bound him, and gouged his eyes out. He was imprisoned, forced to grind at a mill like a slave, walking in blind circles.[119] This is exactly the opposite of what God intended for his life.

We never read that Samson lived a life of worship. His heart was not focussed on God. As Samson had no priestly stance, he was not entrusted with the authority necessary to execute his assignment over the Philistines, rather he was humiliated. God's anointed ones are never to walk blindly in circles. We are to be clothed in righteousness, moving forward with clear vision to serve His Kingdom.

Sadly, Samson will be remembered for his self-centred life, wasted on the altar of pleasure. Only through redemptive grace was he able to kill many Philistines at the moment of his death.[120]

Our personal calling only come into fruition if we live according to the eternal ways of God, and not in our own

---

116.   Judges 14:19; 15:14
117.   Judges 16:20
118.   Judges 13:5
119.   Judges 16:21
120.   Judges 16:28 30

interpretation of it. The manifestation of the Kingdom of God of earth is hindered due to our uncrucified individualism and ego.

Hophni and Phinehas – priests, and sons of Eli

In 1Samuel we find that the Philistines were aggressive. The Israelites had settled in the Promised Land, but had lost the reverence of God's presence dwelling in their midst. Worship in God's tabernacle was polluted and watered-down. Hophni and Phineas were taking personal advantage of the offerings brought to the temple, rebelling against Levitical holiness.

1Samuel 2:7: *The sin of the young men was very great in the sight of the Lord, for the men treated the offering of the Lord with contempt.*

Eli, the high priest, did not deal decisively with their wrongdoings,[121] most probably because he benefitted from their wayward ways. Half-hearted repentance makes the individual feel good, but hinders the Kingdom of God. The spiritual decline in Israel was severe. Israel had no authority among the surrounding nations. They were no longer a testimony to the righteous King on earth. The only true way to triumph over the Philistines in battle, is to live a holy, dedicated life in humble obedience and worship, in self-denial, ministering to God from a heart overflowing with love and gratitude.

As the Israelite army went into battle with the Philistines, they took the Ark of the Covenant with them to soothe their fears and guilty consciences, possibly as an attempt to

---

121.   1Samuel 2:22-25

manipulate God's arm. But the battle was lost, the Ark was taken[122], and eventually restored to Kiriath-Jearim on the margin of Israel.[123] Thank God that the ark was restored to Israel, but only to the periphery, not to the tabernacle of the Lord. For twenty years, Israel and the priesthood continued life as normal, without the presence of God at the heart of this chosen nation.[124]

This fact exposes the state of the heart of Israel. They did not long for His presence, His ways or His glory. Israel was satisfied with the general sense of being special, but zeal for His house did not consume them. Those twenty years must have been spiritually trying for Samuel, as the priests ministered to God and to the nation of Israel, without the presence of God in the Holy Place. Hearts were hardened. Spiritual darkness settled on the nation.

It is in the midst of this spiritual climate that Israel demands a king. It makes perfect sense, as they had lost the understanding of God being enthroned in their midst. They became earthly, carnal, and spiritually blind. They longed to be just like the other nations. God was no longer considered to be the King in their midst.

Saul – the first king of Israel

God commanded Samuel to anoint Saul as king in **1Samuel 9:16**: *About this time tomorrow, I will send you a man from the land of Benjamin, and you shall anoint him to be a prince over my people. He shall save my people from the hand of the Philistines.*

---

122. 1Samuel 4
123. 1Samuel 6:21
124. 1Samuel 7:2

Saul was externally outstanding, and yet he lacked the humble, god-fearing qualities of a priest-king. Similar to Samson, Saul was specifically set apart with the mandate to destroy the Philistines and secure all of the Promised Land for the Israelites.[125]

1Samuel 9:16: *Tomorrow about this time I will send to you a man from the land of Benjamin, and you shall anoint him to be prince over my people Israel. He shall save my people from the hand of the Philistines.*

Did Saul have the heart of worship, the eternal vision, to execute authority over the Philistines, over the inner Self?

Looking back in history, we know that Saul never conquered his own inner-Philistine. He lived an insecure life of jealousy and comparison, with regular outbursts of anger, even oppressed by demonic forces. Saul lived a soulish life for himself and his own fame.[126] A thin layer of religion was maintained throughout his reign, but we do not read that he worshipped regularly. He did not consider the necessity of God's presence as central to his kingdom, and seemingly agreed to an 'empty' tabernacle without the Ark of the Covenant. It is to no surprise that Saul was unable to walk in true spiritual authority. He could not save Israel from the hands of the Philistines, even although he was anointed and set apart for this very task at his coronation.

Saul's first encounter with the Philistines is recorded in **1Samuel chapter 13**. He panicked and made an unlawful sacrifice to God, which led to him losing the favour of God.[127] As the altar is holy unto God, it must be treated with holy fear in eternal ways. Saul was not a Levite, neither a priest, but a king. Fear of God in exact obedience to His

---

125.   1Samuel 14:52
126.   1Samuel 15:18-30
127.   1Samuel 13:8-12

ways are more significant than a sacrifice. Saul's heart was estranged from God, distant and independent, and he acted soulishly. This foolishness to act as a priest led to the kingdom being removed from him.[128]

In **1Samuel chapter 17**, we read about the famous battle with Goliath, an uncircumcised giant. Saul and his army were paralysed with fear and intimidation as they were mocked by this Philistine, lacking true spiritual authority in the spirit. This is the scene in which David is introduced. This little, unknown shepherd boy had only come to the battlefield to deliver provisions; yet, because of his vertical stance before God that was established in his inner life, he possessed spiritual authority over Goliath. He entered the battlefield with only his slingshot and a few rocks. His trust was in God, whom he knew was a zealous King.

What and who are the Philistines in our lives? Who paralyses us with intimidation? How come God does not rule in all members of our lives? God is mocked on our news feeds and social media, in the political, judicial and sociological arenas. Is there a David to fight for His glory in our generation? Or are we cowering backwards in silence and confusion, lacking authority?

Are we prioritising our priestly role in this generation?

The rest of the book of 1Samuel reveals Saul's persecution of David. He no longer focussed on his calling to destroy the Philistines. He had to prove himself over David. David was treated unjustly, and yet, his superior authority was becoming known in Israel and beyond. We take notice that when king Saul was oppressed by an evil spirit, it was David singing Psalms to restore calm and peace.[129]

---

128.   1Samuel 13:13-14
129.   1Samuel 16:22-23

This principle can't remain hidden: vertical adoration to God subdues our enemies.

We find the final days in the life of Saul in **1Samuel chapter 28**. When faced with the Philistine army, rather than being calm, securely rooted in His covenant love, Saul sought wisdom in fear and trembling from a witch at Endor. **1Samuel chapter 31** records the death of Saul and his three sons by the hand of the Philistines.

Just like Samson, Saul was killed and destroyed by the Philistines, although it was God's intention to destroy the Philistines through these mighty warriors. God's ways are frustrated by soulish lives lived separate from His eternal ways.

Jerusalem:
God's Chosen Headquarters

Jerusalem…is the city of the great King.

Matthew 5:35

The earth was created as a dwelling place for the King Eternal. This earthly domain of the King was granted as an inheritance to Adam. Through God's presence with Adam, the world was to move towards its final, divine purposes. At the end of the ages, the angels would announce:

Revelation 11:15: *The kingdoms of this world have become the kingdoms of our Lord and of His Christ, and He shall reign forever and ever!*

Adam lost his inheritance during the fall, and the restoration of this inheritance is an ongoing process of patience and longsuffering on God's part. It begins small and hidden, when God's presence manifests in the midst of His people, until all the kingdoms of this world will become the kingdoms of our Lord.

After the enemy seized the rulership of the world from Adam, God in His wisdom started to reveal His plan for redemption. He set apart for Himself faithful people with whom He could meet in person, talk to, and lead towards His plan. These were individuals like Noah who built the ark whilst interceding for his generation;[130] Abraham, Isaac, and Jacob, our patriarchs; the twelve tribes; and Moses, the humblest man on earth.[131] God was setting apart a people for Himself: **Exodus 6:7:** *Then I will take you for My people, and I will be your God; and you shall know that I am the Lord your God.*

God made known His desire to them:

Exodus 25:8: *Let them make Me a sanctuary, that I may dwell among them.*

---

130. Ezekiel 14:14
131. Numbers 12:3

Once the tabernacle was completed, God became a permanent companion to His people in their sojourning in the wilderness, both as Father, Saviour and Shepherd.

During the reign of king David, God's divine purposes on earth unfolded into a new stage, and a temple was established in which God on earth dwelt as King, not just as Saviour and accompanying Shepherd. The tabernacle was a mobile temple while God's people were journeying through the wilderness, whilst the temple was an established place in the Land of Promise – a permanent throne for His Kingdom on earth.

Apostle Luke quotes in **Acts 15:16,17:** *After this I will return and will rebuild the tabernacle of David, which has fallen down; I will rebuild its ruins, and I will set it up; so that the rest of mankind may seek the Lord, even all the Gentiles who are called by My name, says the Lord who does all these things.*[132]

The Tent of David was erected first in Zion, the place where David intended to build his palace. The city of Jerusalem, the city of Peace, became the headquarters of God's Kingdom and throne on earth, at the heart of all nations, where Solomon would build the first temple.

From **Acts 15:16,17** we learn that this tent of David needs to be rebuild in preparation for Jesus' second coming. It is of urgent importance to understand the principles and significance of David's Tent, as David was king over God's people, although he fulfilled a mystical priestly role. Let's see how this all unfolded.

---

132.   Quoting Amos 9:11

Jerusalem: God's Earthly Headquarters

During Saul's reign, he set up his tent on the outskirts of Gibeah under the pomegranate tree which is at Migron, instead of having a capital city with a palace. He sat *under the tamarisk tree on the height with his spear in his hand and all his servants were standing about him* (**1Samuel 14:2**). Jerusalem was still in the hands of the Jebusites. The Ark of the covenant was in Kiriath-Jearim[133] after its return from the Philistine lords, whilst Samuel travelled between Bethel, Gilgal and Mizpah.[134] The actual Tabernacle, the empty tent, was still in Ephrathah,[135] and eventually moved to Gibeon.[136]

Under the haunting persecution David suffered under Saul, he fled to Ziklag.[137] There he remained until after Saul's death. When David and his men moved to Hebron he was anointed king over the house of Judah.[138] David lived and ruled in Hebron for seven years.

Once David was anointed king over all twelve tribes of Israel in Hebron,[139] he made a definitive move. He immediately entered into battle to conquer the city of Jerusalem.[140] His heart was set on conquering this particular city ruled by the Jebusites.

Let's consider the options in this new king's life: David could have established his residence in any of the places

---

133. 1Samuel 6:21
134. 1Samuel 7:15
135. Psalm 132:6
136. 1Chronicles 16:39
137. 1Samuel 30
138. 2Samuel 2:1-4ᵃ
139. 2Samuel 5:1-5
140. 2Samuel 5:6-10

mentioned above – near the ark of the covenant, or near the tabernacle, albeit without the presence of God. There were also other options. Bethel is the *House of God*,[141] or Beersheba is the well where both Abraham and Jacob dwelt.[142] Bethany, meaning *House of figs*, was a town favoured by Jesus, as He frequented it during His ministry years, always being refreshed in the house of Lazarus and his sisters. David had multiple possibilities to settle and build a temple for the Lord within the Promised Land. Why would he be so single-minded focussed on taking the occupied city of Jerusalem?

Undoubtedly David understood God's eternal ways and purposes. He grasped the prophetic significance of God choosing Jerusalem as a place to dwell on earth:

Psalm 132:13-14: *For the LORD has chosen Zion; He has desired it for His dwelling place: 'This is my resting place forever; here I will dwell, for I have desired it.'*

David understood that his own kingship was only being a representative of God's Kingdom and His divine throne. God was the actual, invisible King residing in their midst as King of all nations.

Therefore David, through a prophetic Spirit of God, chose this city as his capital, and was determined to cast the Jebusites out and possess it. It was of prophetic urgency that God reigns on earth in His chosen abode. David was serving not just his subjects in building an earthly kingdom, but he served eternity in entering the fierce battle to secure Zion, the city of God.[143]

---

141.   Genesis 28:19
142.   Genesis 21:33
143.   Psalm 48:1-2

2Chronicles 6:5-6: *From the day I brought out My people from the land of Egypt I never chose a city from all the tribes of Israel to build a temple where My Name might reside. I never chose any man to become Commander-in-Chief over My people Israel, but I have chosen Jerusalem that My Name may be there, and I have chosen David to be over My people Israel.*

Since the days of Joshua certain pagan nations remained unconquered within the territory of the Promised Land. As such, the Jebusites controlled Jerusalem, the city on the hill.

There are layers of prophetic principles hidden in this mystical battle, principles for the restoration of the world from the domination of the devil. But it becomes clear that the demonic forces understood the significance of Zion, and established a fortress to control this centre of history.

David knew that he had to establish headquarters for God and His Kingdom on earth. This battle with the Jebusites was not simple, as they revelled in the glory of being unconquered for generations. The Jebusites had fortified the place, calling it *the stronghold of Zion*.[144] They were confident that this city could never be seized, and they mocked David and his men, saying that even if those who guarded the stronghold were lame and blind, David would not be able to defeat them! How often the enemy uses insults and ridicule as a strategy to divert God's people, intending to drain our energy and steal our faith. The enemy succeeds if we deem the situation impossible, and give up too early.

We can expect the battle would have been intense. However, David and his men possessed more than just military strategy and fervour. David's inner life of worship and holiness was sealed with authority from heaven. The battle

---

144.   Zion means *'fortress'* or *'stronghold'* in Hebrew

for Jerusalem was a mystical battle won in the heavenlies, taking a beachhead for God's official headquarters on earth. David was burning with jealousy to further God's Kingdom on earth.

Psalm 132:3-5: *I will not enter my house or get into my bed, I will not give sleep to my eyes or slumber to my eyelids, until I find a place for the LORD, a dwelling place for the Mighty One of Jacob.*

Because this was God's plan, as David always inquired of the Lord in all his battles,[145] the Jebusites were conquered, and henceforth the stronghold was called *the City of David*.[146]

What follows gives us insight into the priestly fire that was burning in David, the prophetic burden that determined his life choices. The first thing he did after possessing Zion, was to restore the Ark of the Covenant to the heart of the kingdom. The Ark was the resting place of God,[147] and God's presence was to be in His headquarters. I find it astonishing that David understood not to restore the Ark to the existing tabernacle. David was not walking in the previous chapter revealed on earth. He had prophetic understanding of the unfolding of the next chapter on earth. The tabernacle was the previous stage on earth, of taking the Promised land. Now God was establishing His throne as King on earth. What a man of prophetic insight, walking *in* the divine timing and purpose of God!

David would not reign over God's people without God's presence ruling through him. Eternal worship was to be at the centre of his rulership. This is why the fruit of David's life lasts forever.

---

145. 2Samuel 5:17-25
146. 2Samuel 5:7,9
147. Isaiah 37:16[a]

Zion, also called Jerusalem, became the dwelling place of the King, a big 'tent' on the model of the tabernacle of Moses, i.e. a place where God's people regularly would gather to worship JHWH. Here God would rest on the mercy seat on the Ark, between the cherubim.[148] And from His headquarters God's honour and glory would be proclaimed to all nations.

1Chronicles 15:1ᵇ: *[David] prepared a place for the ark of God and pitched a Tent for it.*

1Chronicles 16:1: *They brought in the ark of God and set it inside the Tent that David had pitched for it, and they offered burnt offerings and peace offerings before God.*

David arranged the ministry of the priesthood in Jerusalem, and organised 24-hour shifts of ongoing worship,[149] and kept a regular morning and evening offering kindled. This remains to be the key behind David's power and authority - to worship the Lord continually.

The prophet Amos calls us to rebuild the Tent of David, to establish His headquarters on earth, no longer physically in Jerusalem, but in multiple nations through the persistent work of priest-kings in the nations. It is impossible for the King to return to the earth without a place to dwell, to establish His earthly throne.

Amos 9:11: *In that day I will raise up the booth of David that is fallen and repair its breaches, and raise up its ruins and rebuild it as in the days of old, the King will not return to the earth without a place to dwell.*

---

148.   Exodus 25:22
149.   1Chronicles 23-27

David - the Worshipper

Who was David? How did his understanding of such everlasting things mature? How was he able to walk in the everlasting ways as a king?

During David's childhood, the ark of God was not present in the tabernacle, but was resting in distant Kiriath-Jearim.

1Samuel 7:2: *From the day that the ark was lodged at Kiriath-Jearim, a long time passed, some twenty years, and all the house of Israel lamented after the LORD.*

David grew up knowing the law of the Lord, but not His manifest presence. This was not only a sad unfolding of history, but a clear deviation of divine objectives.

David was a shepherd boy, the youngest in his family, looking after his family's flock in the wilderness. He learnt from a young age to worship God in loneliness, in danger, and in every season. He was familiar with fighting lions and bears, symbolising spiritual powers – battles bigger than himself. God taught him to fight these demonic powers on his harp whilst singing to the great *I Am* at night, or in the scorching heat during the day. By the time David came into the public eye, he was a trained warrior with a strong inner, vertical stance, and an absolute trust in God burning in his young heart. Actually, he was driven with jealousy for God's glory. This fervour became the compass to direct David in decisions he would have to make in coming decades. David lived from his priestly heart, and he would shape history accordingly.

In **1Samuel chapter 17** David stepped onto the public stage in the confrontation with Goliath. This was not a physical battle of strength, but a spiritual battle of hearts. As he stepped out on to the battlefield, his cry was for God's honour:

1Samuel 17:26: *Who is this uncircumcised Philistine who defies the armies of the living God?*

David refused the military attire, but entered battle only with his sling shot and a few rocks. This was a spiritual battle, a mystical confrontation. In humility he destroyed the powers of evil as Goliath was killed with his own sword. This battle proclaimed David as the Lord's anointed, a forerunner to the Messiah, and he was anointed by the prophet Samuel as king.[150]

David - the King

Psalm 27:4: *One thing I desire from the LORD, that I will seek after: that I may dwell in the house of Jehovah all the days of my life, to behold the beauty of LORD, and to pray in His temple.*

In the book of **2Samuel** we find the magnificent reversal of the sad events of the first chapters of 1Samuel. In the book of **1Samuel** a corrupt priesthood was serving a nation, where each one did as was right in their own eyes.[151] Leadership was lacking. Consecration was absent. And the Presence of God was not treasured.

In **2Samuel chapter 5**, David becomes king over all Israel. As described earlier in this chapter, the intentionality of his inner being is immediately revealed after his coronation in Hebron. The only thing he cared for, was to make his capital the headquarters of God's Kingdom, and to bring the Ark of the Covenant to the heart of his nation.[152]

---

150. 1Samuel 16
151. Judges 21:25
152. 1Kings 13-16

As a result, David, the worshiping warrior, decisively destroyed the Philistines,[153] which both the Nazirite Samson and king Saul failed to do. David possessed inner authority over his ego, a selfless man living for the glory of God, who could defeat the Philistines.

In **2Samuel chapter 6** David brought the Ark of the Covenant, the dwelling Presence of God to Jerusalem. David danced before the procession, wearing a priestly linen ephod, as priest-king.[154] David was a man after God's heart.

Act 13:22: *[God] raised up David to be their king, of whom He testified and said, 'I have found in David the son of Jesse a man after My heart, who will do all My will.'*

This ushers in the period called 'the Tabernacle of David' referred to in Amos 9:11, a time of continuous, abandoned worship, day and night.

In our present theological milieu, I feel it necessary to underline that the worship in the tabernacle of David was not organised, structured intercession of small groups, praying strategically into certain social topics of concern. We find in his Tent worship that was alive unto God alone. Though structured, it was innocent, not calculated. It had a vertical axis in every aspect, filled with joy and adulation, and the fear of God. It was rooted in truth and in history, although reaching into the eternal future to fulfil prophecies. It was not a program run by a central personality, but worship coming from the hearts of a nation unto their God resting and ruling in their midst. Undoubtedly we can assume that each day was framed by humble repentance and gratitude.

---

153.   2Samuel 5:17-25
154.   2Samuel 6:14

The reign of king David was unprecedented in all history. His reign was characterised by material prosperity, and an ever deepening hunger and longing for worship and ministry to God. He conquered all his enemies and occupied the whole land as promised to Abraham in Genesis chapter fifteen. Some of the battles of him and his mighty men are described in **2Samuel chapters 21-23**, most of them supernatural, beyond human capabilities.

2Samuel 8:6: *David put garrisons in Syria of Damascus. And the Syrians became servants to David, bringing gifts. And the LORD gave victory to David wherever he went.*

He completed his battles. Thus, peace prevailed in his kingdom, even into the next generation. There was no need for Solomon to engage in endless battles as his father was.

1Chronicles 17:7-8: *Now you shall say this to My servant David, so says the Lord of Hosts, 'I took you from the pasture, from following the sheep, so that you should be ruler over My people Israel. I have been with you wherever you have walked, and have cut off all your enemies from before you, and have made you a name like the name of the great men in the earth.'*

It comes to no surprise that David desired to build a permanent dwelling place for God in Jerusalem. How consistent were the intentions of his heart! In **2Samuel chapter 7** David started the process of establishing a permanent dwelling place to the Lord in Jerusalem, not just a Tent.[155] David bought the land[156], and did all the detailed preparation and planning for the building,[157] and charged Solomon, his descendant, to build the temple after his death.[158]

---

155. Also 1Chronicles 17
156. 2Samuel 24:18-25
157. 1Chronicles 22-29
158. 1Kings 5 6

Without God's dwelling and ruling Presence in our ministries, we do not have authority to impact spiritual realities in nations. We are only busy, even though we are doing good deeds.

Concluding

† David understood that he was only to be an earthly representative and servant to the transcended King.

† God's heavenly Kingdom should have earthly headquarters to host God's presence, before nations would acknowledge God as King, and worship Him.

† The presence of the Philistines and God's presence can never dwell together. We either live for the one, or the other. We should destroy the enemy, not giving him any room in our lives.[159] **Galatians 5:16:** *But I say, walk by the Spirit, and you will not gratify the desires of the flesh.*

We need the characteristics and focus of such a man of God as David was, who would restore the lost, heavenly inheritance on earth, especially in our generation:

† David was filled with love for God – a worshipper. He gifted all generations with the book of prayer and worship: the Psalms.

† David received the anointing from the Spirit – he did not go about in his own strength or creative initiatives.

---

159.   Romans 6:12

† David was zealous with God's zeal for the people of God.[160]

† Establishing a dwelling place for the King is always costly. David endured much suffering:[161] the jealousy of Saul; the chasing of his son, Absalom etc.

† David fought seemingly impossible battles with daring faith.[162]

† David was sensitive towards God when he sinned. He deeply repented and humbled himself,[163] and was restored in His grace.

---

160. Psalm 132:4
161. Psalm 102:1-11
162. 2Samuel 23:8-39
163. Psalm 51

Zion, the City of Our God

*Great is the LORD and greatly to be praised in the city of our
God!*
*His holy mountain, beautiful in elevation, is the joy of all the
earth,*
Mount Zion, in the far north, the city of the great King.
Within her citadels God has made Himself known as a fortress.
For behold, the kings assembled; they came on together.
As soon as they saw it, they were astounded;
they were in panic; they took to flight.
Trembling took hold of them there,
anguish as of a woman in labour.
By the east wind you shattered the ships of Tarshish.
As we have heard, so have we seen in the city of
the LORD of hosts, in the city of our God,
which God will establish forever.
Selah.
We have thought on your steadfast love,
O God, in the midst of your temple.
As your Name, O God, so your praise reaches to the ends of the
earth.
Your right hand is filled with righteousness.
Let Mount Zion be glad!
Let the daughters of Judah rejoice because of your judgments!
Walk about Zion, go around her, number her towers,
consider well her ramparts, go through her citadels,
that you may tell the next generation that this is God,
our God forever and ever.
He will guide us forever.

Psalm 48

Zion

You are My Son, today I have begotten You.
Ask of Me, and I will give You the nations for Your inheritance,
and the ends of the earth for Your possession.

Psalm 2:8

The words of **Psalm 2** are primarily a prophecy related to the Incarnation of Christ: *You are My Son, today I have begotten You.*

Yet, what do the words in verse 6 mean? *Ask of Me, and I will give You the nations for Your inheritance.* Is there a possible connection between the Incarnation, and the Restoration of our Inheritance in the nations?

The Earth belongs to man

God, as a loving Father, created Adam as His son in an act of love. A son is always given an inheritance! As God's son[164] everything on earth was Adam's inheritance.

Psalm 115:16: *The heaven, even the heavens, are the Lord's; but the earth He has given to the children of men.*

The earth was created to yield abundant food for all its inhabitants. But the fall wounded and distorted creation, so that the earth was restrained from being fully what it was intended to be. [165]

Genesis 4:12ª: *When you till the ground, it will not again give its strength to you.*

Even the animals groan, as they were not created with such beastly natures. The lion and the lamb were created to be friends. Animosity, fear and bloody appetites came about after sin entered creation.

As noticed in previous chapters, Adam lost his inheritance. The enemy seized this inheritance illegally and is now called

---

164.   Luke 3:38
165.   Genesis 3:17-18

the ruler of this world,[166] ruling through death. Ever since then the earth has been longing for the rulership of the true King.

Restoration

God, whose ways and wisdom are beyond time, sent His only begotten Son into the world, incarnated in a divine mystery, to restore the earth under righteous, life-giving authority. Jesus, as the Son of God, unmistakably qualifies for an inheritance.

Galatians 4:4-7: *But when the fullness of the time had come, God sent forth His Son, born of a woman, born under the law, to redeem those who were under the law, that we might receive the adoption as sons. And because we are sons, God has sent forth the Spirit of His Son into your hearts, crying out, 'Abba Father!' Therefore you are no longer a slave but a son, and if a son, then an heir of God through Christ.*

God sent His incarnated Son, who took the same human image as the first Adam upon Himself,[167] to restore the inheritance on earth to mankind.

Once Jesus was proclaimed as the Messiah in His baptism in the Jordan, He began His earthly responsibility to restore the lost inheritance. Jesus began by fasting for forty days. This fast did not only correct Adam's eating of the Tree of Knowledge of Good and Evil; there was much more to it. The fast was to reveal Jesus as 'the second Adam.'[168] The enemy recognised God-in-human-form, and understood

---

166. John 14:30
167. Philippians 2:7
168. 1Corinthians 15:47

that this would be the One who could and would take the inheritance from him. As soon as the enemy saw this God-man, the last Adam, revealed in the Jordan, he moved into action to oppose Jesus through every and all temptations. He began by bargaining with Jesus: *You can have the inheritance, if you submit to me.*

Luke 4:5-6: *Then the devil…showed Him all the kingdoms of the world in a moment of time. And the devil said to Him, 'All this authority I give You, and their glory; for this has been delivered to me, and I give it to whomever I wish.'*

Christ immediately rebuked him, saying: **verse 8** *'Get behind Me, Satan!'*

God sent His Son to restore the lost inheritance not to Himself, but to mankind. Jesus is ultimately the eternal Heir, to whom all things belong eternally,[169] and mankind become co-heirs with Him in His redemption. [170]

Romans 8:17: *If children, then heirs – heirs of God and joint heirs with Christ.*

The story of the Prodigal son[171] is not merely a parable of any wandering man who separates from his father. This story is in actuality about Adam and his descendants, who were separated from their Eternal Father, who were lost in the world and squandered their inheritance. Actually, the concept of squandering is but a euphemism about what we have done to our inheritance. God's salvific desire is to restore mankind to the Father, and to restore the earth as our inheritance.

---

169.   Genesis 14:19; Psalm 89:11
170.   Also Hebrews 1:2
171.   Luke 15

Jesus Restores our Inheritance

The only true authority found in heaven and earth, is found in the King Eternal. All other authority is fake, selfish, and result in pain and shame. The King Himself, the second Person of the Trinity, came to earth, was incarnated, and lived and served for the pleasure of His Father, and for the love of humanity. From the life of this victorious Christ we receive the fruits of His salvation.

Restoration of our corrupted nature

John 1:12: *However, to all who received Him, those believing in His Name, He gave authority to become God's children.*

The use of the word 'authority' in this sentence seems odd. Was it not possible to simply say that *He granted them to become children of God*?

The choice of the word 'authority' implies that the concept of sonship is linked to the restoration of our lost inheritance. Sonship with authority indicates both responsibility, and enablement to rule on earth. Being, or becoming a son, causes battles on earth which would never be accomplished without His authority.

Because of what Jesus prepared for us in salvation, we need Christ to be formed in our inner beings, as He was the God-man, the last Adam who triumphed over the enemy and restored our inheritance. His victory becomes ours as we covenanted with Him in salvation, and yet, it is our privilege AND responsibility to be fully clothed with Christ so that we can inherit what was given to us.

Colossians 3:10: *Put on the new man who is renewed in the knowledge according to the image of Him who created him.*

Ephesians 4:24: *Put on the new man which was created according to God, in true righteousness and holiness.*

Receiving the seed of this new nature in our inner beings is the initial step, and we should continue to cultivate spiritual growth with focus and sacrifice until the new man is fully grown into maturity, until Christ is formed in us.

Galatians 4:19: *My little children, for whom I labour in birth again until Christ is formed in you.*

Only then our inheritance will be actualised, and not just remain a theological ideology.

The Galatians were already believers in Christ, and yet, apostle Paul was labouring in birth pains until Christ was fully formed in them. The same concept is repeated to the church in Ephesus when Paul was praying for these believers *'that Christ may dwell in your hearts'* (**Ephesians 3:17**).

God desires to live within believers in His fullness.[172] Without the indwelling of Christ in our hearts it is not possible to exercise the victory of the restoration of our earthly inheritance. Only as Christ is mystically present within the Church, only then His authority can manifest through us to restore what was stolen.

The enemy loathes losing anything he has deceptively gained, resulting in unceasing wars against the formation of God's Presence within His redeemed. It is no surprise that the enemy hates the children of God who walk circumspectly, treasuring Christ's actual Presence within. Satan views the faithful children of God in the same way he

---

172.   John 14:23; Colossians 2:9-10

viewed Christ in the wilderness. He sees the image of the Son in them, and he trembles. He knows that true sons of God have authority to rule on earth, an honour which he usurped. If Christians truly grow into mature Christlikeness,[173] his dream will be destroyed to possess the earth forever.

Satan rules through the medium of sin, and always concentrates on increasing evil with the purpose to destroy the earth – for Death to rule forever. Sin strengthens Satan's authority if we obey him, but repentance and humility before God restore Adam as heir and ruler on earth.

We should expect resistance and suffering in our spiritual walk. And yet, the hardship counts towards our spiritual formation, for us to become one with the Crucified One, so that the humble but victorious King can reign through us. This will truly annihilate the works of the evil one.

Philippians 3:10-11: *That I may know Him and the power of His resurrection, and may share His sufferings, becoming like Him in his death, that by any means possible I may attain the resurrection from the dead.*

Restoring the earth as our inheritance

The mystery of restoring the earth is closely linked to the previous point. The earth can only be subdued by the children of God who have been transformed into the image of Christ through the blood of Him who gave His life for our redemption. The earth would then once again become the Kingdom of our God, ruled over in righteousness and justice.[174] At the end of the age, the angels will announce the final transferral of authority:

---

173.   Colossians 2:28
174.   Psalm 89:14

Revelation 11:15: *The kingdoms of this world have become the kingdoms of our Lord and of His Christ and He shall reign forever and ever!*

This principle of transferring a kingdom from one power to another is seen in the Old Testament. In **2Kings chapter 5** we find an interesting story. Naaman, a Syrian officer, suffered with leprosy and sought after the prophet Elisha for healing. Once miraculously healed, Naaman presented a strange request to Elisha:

2Kings 5:17: *Then please let your servant load two mules with dirt from Israel, because your servant will no longer offer any burnt offering or sacrifice to any other god but the LORD.*

This is fascinating. The commander of the Syrian army, the Minister of Defence, asked for a load of soil to be carried back to his homeland so that he might worship the God of Israel?! Why did he not simply build an altar on Syrian soil to worship God?

Naaman understood who ruled in Israel, and who ruled in Syria. Syrian land, the actual soil, was dedicated to the pagan gods through many rituals and sacrifices, over many generations. The land was polluted and defiled, belonging to and was ruled by these gods. As Naaman longed to build an altar to the God of Israel, he needed pure soil that would honour the God of Israel. The actual soil of Israel was spiritually different than the soil of Syria, because a different King ruled over this land! The soil of Israel was dedicated to YHWH through centuries of obedience and worship, and as a result the soil was sanctified by His Presence dwelling in this land. Thus, Naaman brought soil from Israel to worship a holy God in Syria. This became his foothold to establish a dwelling place for God within Syrian territory, amidst the ongoing pagan worship.

Our nations, our lands are ruled by Satan, the deceiver, liar and murderer. Our physical lands are dedicated to him through generations of bloodshed, immorality, corruption and injustice, to the point that our actual soil is adulterated and contaminated. [175]

Isaiah 24:5 *The earth is also polluted by its inhabitants, for they transgressed laws, violated statutes, broke the everlasting covenant.*

Altars that offer pure, ongoing, priestly *liturgia* redeem and subdue the actual soil of our lands. Once a place is established for the King to dwell, then the rulership of God will extend in our lands to bring about healing and restoration to our present ecological calamity, even further afield to the seas and the air.

Living holy lives in abiding in His Kingly presence is pivotal to sanctifying the nations, and our lands. Indeed, creation waits with eager expectation for 'the revealing of the sons of God':

Romans 8:19-32: *For the creation waits with eager longing for the revealing of the sons of God. For the creation was subjected to futility, not willingly, but because of him who subjected it, in hope that the creation itself will be set free from its bondage to corruption and obtain the freedom of the glory of the children of God. For we know that the whole creation has been groaning together in the pains of childbirth until now. And not only the creation, but we ourselves, who have the first-fruits of the Spirit, groan inwardly as we wait eagerly for adoption as sons, the redemption of our bodies. The material creation groans in agony, knowing that only the true sons of God can restore it.*

---

175. Numbers 35:33; Leviticus 18:25,27; Ezekiel 36:16-17

However, as we have said, it is not an automatic process.

The Presence of God

According to God's omnipresent nature which fills all in all,[176] we know that God is present everywhere. Yet, we long not only for the general presence of God, but the actual Presence of a Person, as though another Person is present with us. God is a Person. He planned, and is pleased to dwell *in us,* and *among us* through an actual Person-Presence.[177]

The exchange of one kingdom for another requires the fullness of this specific Person-Presence.

The early Church considered His actual Presence within the Church differently than we do today. Our insight is often merely assumed, in that when we worship, He simply comes amongst us. As we taste the comfort of the Holy Spirit in our midst, we belief it to be an indication that God is present amongst us. This results in any spiritual experience often being considered as the 'Presence of God.'

According to the Church Fathers, the true Presence of God has different levels, and has variable effects accordingly. His true and divine Person-Presence requires us to prepare a dwelling place for Him. Also, the Church should have a complete understanding of being united with the Person of God as an indwelling presence. This requires enlightened teaching,[178] as well as a commitment from each believer in the ancient steps of purification (*catharsis*), leading to

---

176.   Ephesians 1:23

177.   Luke 17:21

178.   Father Macarius (Dr Atef Meshreky) explains the theology of salvation as taught and lived by the Early Church in: '*The Inner man & The Formation of Christ.*' ISBN 978 0 9971428 3 9 03230   *www.shineinternational.org*

revelation (*fotisis*), which eventually results in true Union with God the Almighty. Much is written about this process of union with God (*theosis*) in theology.[179]

Divine visitation, or what we often call a general manifestation of His presence, does not dethrone the evil one on earth. A visitation can quicken our hearts to see with a new perspective, or to be healed. Whilst it produces fruit personally, it does not shift the spiritual realm corporately. God loves to encourage, correct and minister to our needs, and therefore history is filled with His gracious visitations. However, we need a true, constant indwelling of His Person-Presence on earth to see His Kingdom come, to restore the world to God's authorative rulership.

Just to underline: Visitations from God produce great and necessary fruit in individual lives, to wake us up, to reveal His purposes for us, to enable us to turn towards Him. But the indwelling of the fullness of God's Presence possesses the land, restoring it from the enemy who has looted and stolen it, resulting in healing and sanctification. Then God's Kingdom can manifest on earth as in Heaven.

A Byzantine saying goes:
The Church is an earthly heaven in which the heavenly dwells and moves.[180]

179.　*Catharsis*: the purification of the heart and mind from egotistical and soulish passions and addictions
Fotisis: the enlightenment of the soul, also called illumination – a gift of the Holy Spirit once the soul has undergone purification, leading to deeper cleansing and sanctification
Theosis: a transformative process of true union with God, partaking in divinity (2Peter 1:4). Man is deified by grace, as taught by the Church Fathers
180.　Germanus, Patriarch of Constantinople, died 733AD

Zion[181]

Eden is no longer God's dwelling place on earth. As we have seen in chapter 9, Zion is God's eternal chosen place to dwell and rule on earth. As it was, so shall it be forever!

Psalm 2:6: *I have set my king on Zion, my holy mountain.*

Zion has been proclaimed by God as His intended headquarters on earth. Once God is enthroned on His holy hill of Zion, the earth will be restored to His rulership. David honoured Zion as the divinely chosen place from where God will establish His Kingdom on earth.

Psalm 68:16: *Why do you gaze in envy, O mountain range, at the Mountain God has chosen for His resting place? Yes, the LORD will dwell in it forever.*

Psalm 102:12-16: *But you, O Lord, are enthroned forever; You are remembered throughout all generations. You will arise and have pity on Zion; it is the time to favour her; the appointed time has come...For the Lord builds up Zion; He appears in His glory.*

These verses were written at a time when Zion was lying in ruins. Yet, the psalmist realised by the Holy Spirit God's special purpose for this place, that *He has desired it...forever.* The Psalmist was awaiting God's visitation, which was ultimately fulfilled on the day of Pentecost.

Jeremiah mentions the same in **Jeremiah 3:14:** *Return, O faithless children, declares the Lord; for I am your Master; I will take you, one from a city and two from a family, and I will bring you to Zion.*

---

181.   'ZION – *Biblical Study and Vision for Ministry*' by Father Macarius (Atef Meshreky) is a fully comprehensive overview of Zion as a dwelling place and a throne for God on earth. ISBN 9798363232831 *www.shineinternational.org*

This passage speaks of a remnant, a faithful few.

In the same passage Jeremiah explains the future:

Jeremiah 3:16,17: *When you have multiplied and been fruitful in the land, in those days, declares the Lord, they shall no more say, 'The ark of the covenant of the Lord.' It shall not come to mind or be remembered or missed; it shall not be made again. At that time Jerusalem shall be called the Throne of the Lord, and all nations shall gather to it, to the Presence of the Lord in Jerusalem, and they shall no more stubbornly follow their own evil heart.*

These verses refer to the return from exile from Babylon on one level. And yet it also contains a prophetic dimension related to Israel and the people of God, according to the words of apostle Paul in **Romans chapters nine and eleven**.

But importantly, there is an added spiritual dimension to these verses according to the Early Fathers. Jerusalem, or Zion, also refers to the human soul on the individual level, and the Church on the corporate level. Zion is no longer a physical building in Jerusalem, but different units of believers who are united in spirit and vision, who fully understand His ways and times. In these Zion units, in these Christ-like believers, His Presence dwells, and His glory shall be seen.[182]

God's mind is the same; it does not change. He is eagerly waiting for us to build spiritual Zion-units in this generation where He can dwell, to gather His scattered people from different nations, from where His rulership can pierce the darkness of our generation. From Zion, He will rule the nations. Isaiah affirms this:

Isaiah 60:1-3: *Arise, shine, for your light has come, and the glory of the Lord has risen upon you. For behold, darkness shall cover the*

---

182.   Psalm 102:16

earth, and thick darkness the peoples; but the Lord will arise upon you and His glory will be seen upon. And nations shall come to your light, and kings to the brightness of your rising.

Another prophetic reference to these Kingdom units, these Zion units, is found in the New Testament:

Acts 15:16-18: *After this I will return, and I will rebuild the Tent of David that has fallen; I will rebuild its ruins, and I will restore it, that the remnant of mankind may seek the Lord, and all the Gentiles who are called by My Name, says the Lord, who makes these things known from of old.*

God desires for the Tent of David to be built and manifested afresh in His church, and in all nations.

The Church

In the writings of the Church Fathers we find repeated references to the Church as 'Zion,' or 'the spiritual Jerusalem.' Zion is the place where the King is not just in residence, but it is His headquarters where His throne is established, and from where He rules and extends His Kingdom.

The first, Apostolic Church was a true Zion; a place for the Lord's Presence among the nations. On the day of Pentecost, the Holy Spirit was poured out upon and within the followers of Jesus, and remained on them in increasing measure. They lived holy lives in the fear of God and in obedience to His commandments, with one Spirit, and one heart. The Lord was present in the Church with manifest Glory. Thus, His Kingdom extended throughout Asia Minor, where pagan peoples were attracted to His presence, even if it meant dying a cruel, martyr's death.

The real Church, the true Zion, consists of those who are mystically united with the Trinity. They are the ones who keep history on course, despite being opposed by the evil one. They move according to a divine plan towards the second coming of Christ.

The church in each generation should discern how the 'ruler of this world'[183] seeks to divert the advancement of the Kingdom of God. Each generation should discern their particular role in history. Past generations deviated from His ways and His wisdom. During the Renaissance (14th century) Europe became rational, and during the Enlightenment (18th century) we became deeply humanistic. The 20th century saw two World Wars, leaving everything in ruins. Despite this, the following generation turned further away from God and His Eternal ways to the extent that we are now known as post-modern, post-truth, and post-Christian. Our generation is individualistic, independent, secular, and severely materialistic. We suffer from irrepressible lusts, with the media shaping and fragmenting the minds of our youth. Demand for freedom has grown to twisted and illogical levels. We suffer from deep-seated confusion, questioning truth to the point of depression and despair. Our generation is in great need of salvation.

God's ways for us, our only hope, is for Zion-units to be established in the nations, where God can dwell on earth to reach the agonising and desperate with His light and healing.

The enemy is terrified of the manifestation of a true spiritual Zion, a dwelling place of the King on earth. Throughout centuries he tried to deceive the true Church. Divisions and

---

183.   John 12:31

heresies entered, and the character and spirit of the Church metamorphosed. The message of the Gospel was diluted and fragmented, gradually lost. Partial truth produced immature followers, vulnerable for further lies and false teachings. Believers are bound in chronic sin patterns, and lack the knowledge or the desire to be transformed into His glory.[184] The Church lost the vision of restoring the inheritance of the nations. Instead, we became a place for individualistic comfort.

Our generation is very poor in a true vision of His Kingdom.

But all is not lost. Never. Thanks to God's steadfast love that endures forever, there will always be a remnant, a faithful few, in the words of prophet Isaiah: *a handful of corn*.[185] Through them, God's purposes are re-established on earth, even in our generation. These faithful ones will love the Lord and long for Him. And God will entrust Himself to them. This remnant will complete their battles against all lusts and passions, against the ego and self, and with the spirit of the world. Patiently, even though suffering will increase, they will overcome the evil one. They may cry out: *Let this cup pass me!* Yet, love will finally triumph, and they will say: *Not my will, but Your will.*[186]

Philippians 1:21: *For to me to live is Christ, and to die is gain.*

God will gather these individuals together into small Zion-units where His glory will rest, and He will restore and rule the earth. There will be various communities throughout the nations, who will lovingly host His presence in a pure way, and will restore their land to His kingship and authority

---

184.   2Corinthians 3:18
185.   Psalm 72:16 (KJV)
186.   Luke 22:42

through holiness and suffering. God will mystically unite these true Zion units in the nations through His Spirit, and knit these Kingdom units together to become a great net in the nations, who will gather in the harvest in the End Times (chapter 11).

Those who seek truth and deliverance in this dark hour on earth, will be led to these Zion units, and be restored by His Life-giving presence. The Great Commission and task of evangelism[187] cannot be accomplished except through this mystery of Zion units throughout the nations. Time is short, and the workers are few. Many have not heard the message of salvation, and many aggressively reject and despise the Gospel. This is God's prophetic, divine way for completing and fulfilling His commandment through the Church. The authority and reign of God will extend, and nations will be shaken and drawn to repentance and worship.

Yet, there is more. As Zion units are built, as the King is practically resident again in our midst, the earth will truly be restored as our inheritance. Only then, the final scene of His Second Coming can be inaugurated.

May the eyes of our hearts be opened to see that the world has forcefully sent Jesus out of its midst. They reject Him, and mock Him. Even the countries with a historic Christian history and heritage, now actively pursue estrangement from Him, considering Him and His people a disgrace. In response to this, may we burn with holy zeal for the throne of Christ to be restored to His world which He created for Himself.[188]

John 2:17: *Zeal for Your House will consume Me.*

---

187.   Matthew 28:19,20
188.   Colossians 1:16; John 1:10

How immense is the groaning in the heart of Jesus as He desires to be incarnated anew within our hearts and lives, to dwell in places prepared for Him. We recognise His groaning in His intercessory prayer the night before His crucifixion, as repeatedly mentioned in the Gospel of John:

John 17:21,22,25: *The world has not known You…so that the world may know that You sent Me.*

Will we be the ones to usher Him into the world again to rule from within our hearts?!

As in any war, taking occupied land requires a beachhead. The warfare is intense, in our minds, our emotions, our belief systems and mind-sets, and in society. This requires a clear vision to even enter into this battle.

The fullness of the vision of Kingdom of God on earth will never be achieved without New Zion units. Any ministry or calling which lacks the vision to host the Presence of the King as a divine strategy, will be hindered from reaching our true prophetic fullness and fruitfulness.

I do not primarily refer here to religious ministries, but especially to the broader scope of life: to families raising children, boards and companies aiming at having a godly and lasting influence in engineering and technology, in ecological restoration, or *kindergarten* classes, in government, and in the medical field. Whenever, and wherever, we long to see His Kingdom principles manifest through us, it requires us to build a Zion. Serving His Kingdom is not sufficient. He should reign through us.

The Kingdom of God cannot be established on earth unless we build a city for God, headquarters for the King, Zion in our midst. The King requires an earthly throne.

Stages in
Establishing a Zion

Whether a person builds on this foundation with gold,
silver, expensive stones, wood, hay, or straw,
the workmanship of each person will become evident,
for the day of judgment will show what it is,
because it will be revealed with fire,
and the fire will test the quality of each person's action.
If what a person has built on the foundation survives,
he will receive a reward.
If his work is burned up, he will suffer loss.
However, he himself will be saved,
but it will be like going through fire.

1Corinthians 3:12-15

We are dependent on our *Satnav's* to reach our various destinations in many cities and nations. We even follow the instructions in a mindless way. We turn left if told so, and we go straight until new instructions are given. If we disobey, it clearly makes it's emotionless, monotone voice heard, and then re-routes us on the shortest possible path, keeping us on track towards the planned destination.

As we venture through another 100 years of history, we realise that we did not always walk straight. Mankind is short-sighted. Yet, we have the divine *Satnav* of the eternal voice of God who redirects us, recalculating our journey if we got lost. Importantly, we have history to lean on, to encourage us to keep going forward. Just as a *Satnav* calmly redirects us without frustration or disappointment, so does God, although not in an impersonal, robotic way. There is constant guidance leading us forward, unless we cut ourselves off from His voice. God always speaks to mankind. God told Israel to stop going around the mountain as He led them towards the Jordan.[189] He gave detailed instructions on the building of the tabernacle.[190] And God brought the remnant back from Babylon to rebuild Jerusalem and the temple.[191]

Isaiah 30:21: *Your ears shall hear a word behind you, saying, 'This is the way, walk in it,' when you turn to the right or when you turn to the left.*

On this long journey through history to see His Kingdom on earth, we hold on to the ultimate understanding that Jesus is coming to restore everything.

---

189.   Deuteronomy 1:6-8
190.   Exodus 24
191.   Nehemiah and Ezra

Revelations 21:5ᵃ: *He who was seated on the Throne said, 'Behold, I am making all things new.'*

Each step, each phase is entrusted and revealed to each generation in prayer. We cannot afford to function separately from previous generations, as all is built together until complete perfection is reached.

The following pages are overlapping with the previous two chapters, but with a different angle, to highlight God's patient unfolding of His supreme will on earth through the ages.

Three Phases[192]

1. During the **Old Testament** the Kingdom of God was a hidden reality.
2. During the **New Testament** the Kingdom of God was revealed in the hearts of believers.
3. In the **Age to Come** the Kingdom of God will publicly manifest to the whole world: unbelievers and believers alike.

The Kingdom of God in the Old Testament

After the Fall, the public and bright manifestation of the Kingdom of God was lost. Instead, the kingdom of death was established through the rule of the Evil One through demonic strategies of jealousy, greed, hatred and murder, always with the purpose to destroy and kill.

---

192.   This understanding is in detail described in *'Kingdom of God & The End Times'* by Father Macarius (Dr Atef Meshresky) – used with permission. ISBN 979 11 86606 00 1 03230 *www.shineinternational.org*

In the next phase, the Kingdom of God manifested first in the lives of the **Patriarchs.** The Kingdom of God was hidden, and personal. **Noah** offered sacrifices when he came out of the ark. God told him that He would never again curse the land, nor destroy every living creature through water.[193]

God also appeared to **Abraham** at Moreh several times.[194] **Isaac** and **Jacob** also encountered God. In **Genesis 28:16-19** Jacob awoke from his dream to realise that the Lord was right there. He called that place the House of God, the gate of Heaven - Bethel. The Kingdom of God was a hidden manifestation on personal altars, although very real. God's throne and authority was not yet visible in the nations.

Moses, with the law and the sacrifices, is central to the next phase on earth. The Ark of the Covenant was the Throne of God on earth, as God dwelt between the cherubim on the mercy seat, to meet with His people.[195]

The manifestation of His Kingdom advanced in each phase on earth. The destruction and damage that the Fall caused in lives and society meant that no-one could bear to behold God's glory. Anybody would have been killed due to its brilliance and holiness. Therefore, we find no direct references to His glory in the lives of Adam, Noah and Abraham, as the Law (the priesthood, the sacrifices, and the ark with the mercy seat) was needed to cover the results of the Fall. But, in the tabernacle of Moses, for the first time since Eden, mankind saw openly the glory of God as the cloud covered the tent of meeting.[196]

---

193. Genesis 8:21
194. Genesis 12:6-13
195. Exodus 33:7,9
196. Exodus 40:34-35

As Israel journeyed through the wilderness, the manifestation of the Kingdom of God was visible for the people of the covenant, and even for neighbouring nations, who trembled at His presence. His Kingdom was visible with the human eye, and also clearly discerned in the accompanying blessings, prosperity, provision, health and security that God extended in His loving accompaniment: *If you obey My laws, I will bless you.*[197]

It is important to understand the phases, the stages of progressive manifestation of the Kingdom of God on earth. During the first stage of the Patriarchs from Adam to Abraham, God was teaching them to have fellowship with Him through priesthood.

In the second phase, represented by the tabernacle, God covered sin and the consequences of the Fall. Only forgiveness made it possible for His glory to manifest openly on earth. Any true manifestation of the Kingdom of God is always accompanied with the glory of God. These two elements are actually one. And our hearts should long for the fullness thereof. This is true and complete salvation.

John 17:22: *I have given them the glory that You gave Me, so that they may be one, just as We are one.*

In the third phase of the manifestation of God's Kingdom on earth, we look at Jerusalem. **David** lived his life as a worshipper, and God revealed everlasting mysteries to him. He understood that the earthly king is only representing the heavenly King on earth. His capital became the place where the heavenly King resided – God's earthly headquarters.

---

197.   Deuteronomy 28:1-13

The Presence of God was no longer in a tent, moving around in the wilderness. The Throne of God became an established place with foundations on the Mountain of the Lord, and His glory manifested publicly - **1Kings 8:10-11**. God's glory shone forth, even reaching the Queen of Sheba who came to explore such greatness. The wealth of nations was brought to Zion. There was peace, and old enemies respected Israel.

The purpose of the Temple was always for God to encounter His people, not just individually, but corporately as a nation. The Temple was not just about sin, and sacrifices.[198] God longs to seal His people with His glory. Feast days and sacrifices were means to prepare the nation for an ongoing, holy encounter which would reveal Him to all nations. There was little value in the temple rituals as such, if their hearts were not turned towards God.

Eventually the Jews began to worship the actual temple, and they no longer encountered the Lord of the temple. When Israel was exiled, the temple lost the Presence of God, and His glory lifted from Zion.[199] The nation did not turn their heart towards God, but was led into captivity as slaves to Babylon. The land of Israel was subdued, and without land God could not manifest as King. He became once again a hidden God.

Although the nation returned after 70 years and rebuilt Jerusalem and the Temple, the glory of God did not return. All the Jews could hold on to were the promises of the coming Messiah.

---

198.   Leviticus 8 and 9
199.   Ezekiel 10

The Kingdom of God in the New Testament

Jesus began His public ministry after returning from the wilderness by proclaiming Himself as King:

Matthew 4:17: *From then on, Jesus began to preach, 'Repent, because the kingdom from heaven is near!'*

This same proclamation was entrusted to the disciples, and it became the foundation of the ministry of the Apostles.[200] It becomes clear that experiencing the Kingdom of God on earth comes about only through repentance. There is no other way to pursue and build the Kingdom of God, but through deep and revelatory repentance that washes away the old idolatry, the corruption and damage of sin, and the entanglement of the spirit of the world. Repentance is the first step to establish His Kingdom in our own hearts, and in our nations. This was the message of John the Baptist,[201] the message of Jesus,[202] and the message handed down to His twelve disciples.[203] After the Resurrection, in the book of Acts, as the apostles preached the death and resurrection of the Messiah, they called all to repentance.[204]

In this phase, the Kingdom of God is a manifestation of the work of the Blood of Jesus in our inner lives, before it can overflow into society. That is the underlined difference between true spiritual, missionary work in serving nations; and secular, humanitarian work trying to better society.

We link repentance to confession of sin, and the renewal of our minds – which is true. But if repentance is not

---

200.   Luke 6:20
201.   Matthew 3:2
202.   Mark 1:15
203.   Mark 6:12
204.   Acts 2:38; 17:30

linked with the reign of Christ in our lives, confession of sin and repentance remain to be incomplete. In such a case we ongoingly struggle with recurring sins, resulting in chronic frustration, even despair, and His reign continues to suffer in the generation. Repentance is completed when His rulership, His throne is established in every area of our lives. When we start to experience that, He fights our spiritual battles on our behalf. Then we will conquer sin. And His glory will truly rest upon us, and within us. Only then His Kingdom will be proclaimed through our lives in all actuality, not by faith alone.

At the beginning of Jesus' ministry, He proclaimed that the Kingdom of God is at hand. Towards the end of His earthly ministry, after three years, as He approached the cross, He preached that *'the Kingdom of God is within you'* (**Luke 17:21**). There is a vast difference in these two proclamations. Jesus had laboured in the heart of His disciples, and He was now officially announcing a new phase on earth. The Kingdom is no longer near, but actually within us.

On the day of Pentecost, the Kingdom of God began to extend into the nations, and the Church was born within the apostles. The Church became the spiritual Zion[205] - the dwelling place for His presence and His glory on earth. The Church Fathers taught that inside each person is a spiritual Jerusalem with hidden glory.[206] Wherever they moved, the Kingdom of God moved with them, as in the days of Moses and the tabernacle in the wilderness.

The Church is to be the Throne of the King on earth, not just theologically, but practically. His Lordship should be renewed daily in our lives. St Macarius the Great (4th

---

205.   Hebrews 12:18-24
206.   1 Corinthians 3:16

century AD) commented on the vision of God we find in Ezekiel chapter one saying: *The prophet was viewing the mystery of the human soul that would receive His Lord, and become His throne of glory.*

The measure of the manifestation of His Kingdom on earth is directly related to the level of holiness and abiding within the church.[207]

God's glory is always linked to the rulership of God in our lives. If and when all my life is under God's control, once He is the Lord in all areas of my life, then He can entrust His glory. Whilst we struggle to surrender, we hinder the manifestation of His kingdom and His glory in my own life, and in our generation.

True evangelism is when His bright glory shines and attracts others to Himself. The manifestation of His glorious Kingdom will be seen by others, and the world will know that He has sent us:

John 17:23: *I in them and You in Me, that they may become perfectly one, so that the world may know that You sent Me and loved them even as You loved Me.*

The glory of God seals our unity with God, and anoints the commissioning of Christ in us so that all the world will know Him. His glory will unite the Church in His Lordship, and we will shine bright in society.

Matthew 5:14: *You are the light of the world. A city set on a hill cannot be hidden.*

Who can withstand the Presence of the Ultimate King?

---

207.   2Corinthians 6:14 – 2Corinthians 7:1

The different phases of the manifestation of the Kingdom of God in history are constantly continuing to unfold. As in the days of the Patriarchs, God's presence and rulership now dwells within individuals in the Church, without the nations being able to see it with their physical eyes, although they may possibly perceive His presence and grace.

God never changes His mind. He remains true to who He was, and is and always will be. He only adapts His plans in history to different phases and stages. Each time and each generation has a particular *economy*.[208] In the time of the patriarchs His glory was hidden. In the Tabernacle His glory was visible, and in the Temple the Kingdom was established with foundations.

In the New Testament the Kingdom manifested within human beings in a hidden way. The glory upon the Church is not 'seen', and yet it extended into the nations.

When the New Jerusalem comes from above, His Kingdom will be established on twelve foundations, with the public display of His glory emanating from it to the effect that there will be no need for the sun.[209] And every knee and every tongue will confess that He is Lord,[210] both believers and unbelievers. His Kingdom will be openly proclaimed and seen.

If we lack the understanding of God's *economia* through the ages, we may aim to 'fix' the issues of our generation, when we are really called to host the King in our midst, who will restore all and everything. Then the rest will fall into place.

---

208.   Strong's Concordance: **G3622** οἰκονομία, *administration* (of a household or estate); specifically a (religious) 'economy' - dispensation, stewardship. This depicts God's plans, purposes and ways.
209.   Revelation 21:9-21
210.   Philippians 2:10-11

Matthew 6:33: *But seek first the kingdom of God and his righteousness, and all these things will be added to you.*

The Kingdom of God in the Age to Come

In the Age to come, His Kingdom and His glory will be a public manifestation.[211] The appearance of the King, the Ancient of Days, will be for all to see. All corruption and crookedness will be dealt with. His sanctifying presence, His life-giving rule, will renew creation. Death will be destroyed.

The Jerusalem coming from above is being established in heaven right now. Once completed, it will manifest on earth. Because of the resurrection and ascension of Christ, believers in Jesus are raised up with Him and seated in heavenly places.[212] Every believer has two places: one on earth, and one in heavenly realms. On earth, the Holy Spirit builds believers into the Church:

1Peter 2:5: *You, too, as living stones, are building yourselves up into a spiritual house and a holy priesthood, so that you may offer spiritual sacrifices that are acceptable to God through Jesus, the Messiah.*

We are living stones both on earth, and in heaven; being built into the new Jerusalem who will host and display His glory in His second coming. As His glory rests within our lives through purification and sanctification, shining bright in all eternity, we become, not just living stones, but precious stones.

---

211. Daniel 7:13-14
212. Ephesians 2:6

Once this heavenly building is completed, it will be a living city and appear at the time of the Second Coming of Christ, bringing an end to this present age.

Revelation 21:10-11: *He carried me away in the Spirit to a large, high mountain and showed me the holy city, Jerusalem, coming down from God out of heaven. The glory of God was its radiance, and its light was like a valuable gem, like jasper, as clear as crystal.*

Often, as we talk about this Grand Finale, we have a tendency towards passivity. It seems too magnificent, too distant to grasp. The struggle to live holy lives daily is simply too demanding on us to consider the New Jerusalem. Meditating on the grandeur of the new earth and the New Jerusalem will fill us with hope to hasten the Day of His return, the Day of the glorious manifestation of His Kingdom to earth – to see the King reigning on a new earth.

The Kingdom Map

Just as the physical world is mapped, in the same way we find a spiritual map, portraying the divine purposes according to God's will for all times. This *World Salvation Map* portrays divine centres (New Zion units), places prepared and established for the King to dwell and rule on earth. In the fullness of time the Lord will knit all the hidden Zions in the nations together. These units are not related to any denomination, or a particular nation, but are a pure work in the hearts of those who sought Him with all their hearts, minds, and lives. These are the ones who sacrificially[213] built a throne for the King in their midst, united with His glory. God will connect these different

---

213.   Psalm 132:4 5

Kingdom centres into a great fishing net that will be cast into the ocean of the world, the nations, to gather the final harvest. Each Kingdom unit will be an anchoring point on earth, while the connections between the units will form a net. Each Zion unit will be built and tested by the Holy Spirit, each deeply rooted and established with strong foundations, having the capacity to carry much weight, even in storms.

This End Time net will catch fish beyond capacity, and yet will not tear. This net will hold the precious harvest of the lost, and bring it to the shores of eternity.

At the start of Jesus' ministry we read about a miraculous catch of fish in **Luke 5:1-11,** when He called the first disciples to leave all and follow Him, to become fishers of men. They left the catch there on the shore, and followed Jesus. The second time we read about a miraculous catch is in **John chapter 21**, after the Resurrection of Jesus, just before He ascended to heaven. In both stories, the faithful toiled all night, but caught nothing. These events reveal the failure and desperation that result from human attempts in ministry. The disciples have used all their abilities and expertise, worked all night, with little to proof. Sound familiar? Human endeavour, effort and ego can never achieve salvation and make way for the Kingdom of God on earth.

We are so accustomed to disappointment, with regrouping and mending the nets, to sail again with hope, even just for a small catch. We are unable to 'see' with our inner eyes the eternal ways, the *economia* of God for all nations.

At His word, at the right time, according to His eternal ways, He will command the *World Salvation Net* to be revealed in the sea of the world. The result will be astonishing. Because of God's presence, this net will attract many to salvation from within the storms on earth. The net will not tear, but will hold the End Time catch and bring it safely home.

Although the devil is focused on reaching his goal of subduing the nations, this *World Salvation Net* of distinct divine centres with a true, indwelling King, is being formed through the Holy Spirit in the nations. Oh, how glorious!

May we surrender our lives to His eternal ways, and work with the Holy Spirit to see His Kingdom come in our generation.

Practical Steps

A Temple for the Lord

*You know that you are God's sanctuary
and that God's Spirit lives in you, don't you?
If anyone destroys God's sanctuary, God will destroy him,
for God's sanctuary is holy.
And you are that sanctuary!*

1Corinthians 3:16-17

Right at the start of Jesus' ministry He revealed to His disciples His desire for all to become temples of the Lord.

John 2:19: *Jesus answered them, 'Destroy this temple, and in three days I will raise it up.'*

Jesus fulfilled the Old Testament law and all its requirements by becoming the perfect sacrifice for us. As the curtain in the temple was finally torn in His crucifixion, history made a definite turn. After the resurrection Jesus appeared to the disciples in the upper room, and gave them His Spirit.

John 20:21-22: *Jesus told them again, 'Peace be with you. Just as the Father has sent Me, so I am sending you.' When He had said this, He breathed on them and told them, 'Receive the Holy Spirit.'*

The new dispensation has been opened up. From now on, the followers of Jesus Christ will be the carriers of the Presence of God on earth. No longer will His Presence dwell on the Ark of the Covenant behind the curtain in the temple. The believers, once again, through the redemption of our Saviour, have been restored to what the first Adam was created to be: hosting the fullness of the Presence of God in our human bodies, for the Kingdom to manifest on earth, as it is in heaven.

It is God's utmost heart's desire to dwell in mankind, and make His home within us.

John 14:23: *If anyone loves Me, he will keep My Word, and My Father will love him, and We will come to him and make Our home with him.*

Prophetically speaking, the soul of mankind is seen as a land. The soul was taken from the earth in creation. God took the dust of the earth and breathed His own Life into it, and Adam became a living soul. Yet, every land has a ruler. This is fundamental in all wars throughout the ages, as we fight to protect, or increase rulership over our land.

Who rules over the land of my soul? Apostle Paul enlightens us in **Romans 6:12**, as we read that Sin rules in our flesh, in our souls. After the Fall, death entered creation, even entered into man to gain authority over the soul, which encompasses our bodies, emotions, will, and personality.

However, through the gracious work of the Holy Spirit, the process of salvation and sanctification begins within the human spirit, which resides within the soul. Yet, the soul remains under the control of sin. Unless we work out our salvation,[214] bringing all soulish areas of our lives into His light, and under His reign, the indwelling presence of God will be restricted to the spirit only, even for the full duration of one's life. In this case the humble, grace-filled Presence of God within a person can be seen as being imprisoned within the dominating, uncrucified, self-centred soul.

Our desire, and much more the desire of God Himself, is that the spirit should grow, extend, be broadened and deepened for an ongoing increase of Christ-in-me, the hope of glory,[215] until His presence overflows into all of my soul and flesh.[216] For this to happen, the soul surrounding the spirit, the soil of the heart, needs to be weeded, ploughed and deeply sanctified.[217] The completion of the formation of Christ in my inner being depends on this.[218]

---

214. Philippians 2:12
215. Colossians 1:27
216. 1Thessalonians 5:23
217. Matthew 13:1-23
218. In Part 2 of *'The Inner man & The Formation of Christ'* Father Macarius (Dr. Atef Meshreky) expounds this process of salvation:
ISBN 978 0 9971428 3 9 03230 *www.shineinternational.org*

The formation of Christ, the actuality of the indwelling presence of God Himself, can be viewed in exactly the same way as a baby is being formed in the womb. In this analogy, the womb is the spirit within the soul. The seed of salvation is received as a small seed, like a zygote, which longs to grow into a full being. Christ-in-me is like a newly conceived foetus – very real, and eternal, and yet small and nearly insignificant in the decisions and choices I make each day in the overpowering strength of my old nature and established mind-set. As we humbly journey on the road of discipleship, this new internal Life has the potential to grow in becoming a baby, a toddler (untrained and emotional, leading to unstable Christian behaviour), a teenager (confident, yet not wise), and ultimately Christ-in-me can mature into fullness.

Ephesians 4:13: *Until we all attain to the unity of the faith and of the knowledge of the Son of God, to mature manhood, to the measure of the stature of the fullness of Christ.*

Apostle John unpacks this in **1John 2:12-14** when he addresses the different stages of spiritual growth: little children, young men, and fathers, naming the different characteristic of each of these spiritual stages. The difference between an infant and his father lies both in their emotional capacity and physical ability to carry responsibility with wisdom, and is never disputed in real life. In the spiritual life these differences are similarly vast, and determine the capacity to host God's presence, and to serve His Kingdom purposes. The focus is not on the external possibilities of callings and ministries, but rather the internal maturing and growth of the One who humbly desires to abide within mankind. He wants to rule over all of my inner land, both the spirit and soul, the personality and gifts, my relationships and career, my finances, and even my free evenings. He is King, and He is worthy to be enthroned within all the members of my body.[219]

Sadly, there still remain areas of the old man in the land of our souls where sanctification has not yet renewed my old nature. In these areas we find seeds of evil, even roots of sin. Since sanctification has not yet been extended to these areas, God's life-giving rulership has not brought complete restoration yet. This can be compared to a neighbouring land taken by God in war – His Kingdom flag is waving on the flagpoles, yet the actual soil of the land still carries the footprints of the previous reign, covered in pollution and debris, poisonous chemicals and oil spills. The land belongs to the King, and yet the soil is still dead. This is the distress expressed by Apostle Paul in **Romans 7:18-20:** *For I know that nothing good lives in me, that is, in my flesh. For I have the desire to do what is right, but I cannot carry it out. For I don't do the good I want to do, but instead do the evil that I don't want to do. But if I do what I don't want to do, I am no longer the one who is doing it, but it is the sin that is living in me.*

Sin dwells in the soil of the inner land. It reigns in its members.[220] The Holy Spirit wants to halt the deadly effect of sin by ploughing and weeding our inner land. We can plant the cross in our inner lands to cleanse the fleshly corruption and pollution, until the actual soil of our soul is healed, restored, and dedicated to the rulership of the new King, becoming alive and fruitful again. Until this process is complete, the evil one will look upon our lives and say: 'This is my land; this is my dirty signature. This is where I rule!' even if the flag of the King is already planted in our lives.

---

219. Romans 6:13,19
220. Romans 6:11-13

Satan had no rule over the soul or body of Christ while He was on earth.

John14:30ᵇ: *... for the ruler of this world is coming, and he has nothing in Me.*

Satan never had any imprint in Jesus' life, not even a slightest fingerprint. There is no trace of his work in Christ. The fullness of God dwelt in Christ bodily, in His spirit and soul, as He never disobeyed, rebelled, sinned, or yielded to temptation. Every inch of His body, soul and spirit was submitted and united with God Himself.

We too have the privilege and calling to be filled with Christ in similar measures, until His righteousness keeps us from demonic authority. We have been given the ability to say 'no' to sin, to walk in humility and righteousness, through the grace given to us in our Redeemer.

Titus 2:11-12: *For the grace of God has appeared, bringing salvation for all people, training us to renounce ungodliness and worldly passions, and to live self-controlled, upright, and godly lives in the present age.*

This is our daily challenge. If we don't plough our inner lands and sanctify them, we face ongoing demonic interferences and difficulties.

True joy is birthed from the presence of Christ.[221] If the Person of Christ is truly present in our inner beings in His fullness, we will experience a joy unlike any we have ever experienced, the joy of the Kingdom of God.

---

221.   John 16:22-24

Romans 14:17: *For the Kingdom of God is …. righteousness and peace and joy in the Holy Spirit.*

A Temple for the Lord

The Early Church Fathers held the Old and New Testament as parallel revelations. Whereas the outworking of the purposes of God in the Old Testament is material, the New Testament is spiritual. In the Old Testament, we find a physical and tangible temple, which mirrors our inner temples, the place where God longs to dwell.

1Corinthians 3:16-17: *You know that you are God's sanctuary and that God's Spirit lives in you, don't you? If anyone destroys God's sanctuary, God will destroy him, for God's sanctuary is holy. And you are that sanctuary!*

What is the correlation between the material temple of the Lord in Israel, and our inner spiritual temples?

To become a Zion in this generation, a place where His presence really dwells with authority, from where His glory is proclaimed into the nations, we are invited to ongoingly renovate and dedicate our inner sanctuaries to the King.

Although the temple of the Lord in the Old Testament was designed and built with the most extraordinary detailed beauty, God allowed it to be destroyed and burnt to the ground, because of ongoing sin in Israel. Despite much warning over generations, the call to return to God was often neglected, and the neighbouring enemies looted the temple multiple times. Under the revelatory leadership of some kings (like Josiah[222] and Hezekiah[223]), with guidance provided from the prophets, the temple was rebuilt and restored a few times, only to be neglected again by future generations. Eventually the Assyrians completely flattened Zion and the temple. After the return from captivity in Babylon, the temple was rebuilt once more. It stood in Jerusalem until it was finally destroyed in the year 70AD.

This was never God's intention, nor His desire. He wanted Israel to be a steadfast nation, sheltering under His wings with trust and humility, walking in His ways, for His glory in and upon Zion to be proclaimed to other nations, to draw the Gentiles near Him in jealousy, to discover the God of Israel for themselves. Yet, instead of a progressive increase of peace and righteousness, Israel fluctuated in their commitment to God, until they completely lost the divine glory, which was not restored after their return from Babylon. What a sad reality!

Why did God allow this to happen to His sanctuary, His own chosen, dwelling place?

We learn from the material reality in the Old Testament that the temple of the Lord was always vulnerable to attacks. Our inner temples too are prone to attacks and neglect, unless we watch carefully and jealously over His presence in our lives to increase, until established.

The Enemy Fears the Temple

The reason why the evil one hates the temple is clear: the ark represents the throne of God on earth. The enemy knew

---

222. 2Kings 23
223. 2Chronicles 29-31

that if he could interfere with its ongoing worship and even destroy the temple, God would no longer be resident in Israel, and he could restrict and interfere with God's rule on earth. This would open the field for the evil one to extend his deadly rule into nations in an unrestrained way.

Exactly the same principles and truth apply to our inner, spiritual temples. The enemy knows, even more than the church does, that if a believer keeps his temple clean, sanctified and filled with the presence of God, this person will become a hindrance, a real threat to him and the expansion of his dark kingdom. The Presence of Christ within mankind reminds Satan of the absolute defeat on Golgotha, and that his reign on earth has been conquered.[224] This frightens him dreadfully.

The enemy's main strategy remains to ruin the inner temples of believers, to infiltrate the holy places with sin and the spirit of the world, so that the rulership of God in each believer is constrained. If Satan can blind, confuse and pollute the Church at large, the authority of the King is limited on earth, once again. Believers no longer shine brightly on earth, and therefor darkness prevails. Much intellectual theology replaced the actual, bright Presence of God Himself in the Church.

2Thessalonians 2:6-7: *You know what it is that is now holding him* [the lawless one] *back, so that he will be revealed when his time comes. For the secret of this lawlessness is already at work, but only until the person now holding it back gets out of the way.*

It is the responsibility of the Church, not only to restrain the evil one, but to proclaim and extend God's Kingdom on earth until its public manifestation. However, it all

---

224. Colossians 2:15

stands and falls on one single issue: watching over our inner temples.

God calls to us to build and dedicate our inner temples. Each one needs to start with himself and build his or her own inner temple, the altar, the fire burning all day, regular repentance, and much incense to our God, so that the King is able to draw near and increase His dwelling in us, to establish His throne within us. Then the whole Church would be sealed with His Kingship and authority, and His glory will lead many to repentance and salvation in the nations.

Dedicating our Inner Temple

King Hezekiah was a pious and godly king in Judah. His predecessors had worldly concerns and little spiritual interest, but even explored heathen worship. The practice of those worldly kings corrupted the nation of Israel, both the people and the land. The temple of the Lord was tainted, the priestly ministry in the temple ceased, and the temple was used for the worship of pagan gods. Already in the first year of his reign, king Hezekiah opened the doors of the temple (which were closed by king Ahaz[225]) to restore the temple and the priestly ministry:

2Chronicles 29:3: *In the first year of his reign, in the first month, he opened the doors of the house of the Lord and repaired them.*

The primary issue on king Hezekiah's to-do list, straight after his coronation, was to repair the dwelling place of the heavenly King in Jerusalem. Oh, is it possible for our modern nations to again be led by God-fearing leaders who understand eternal principles!

---

225.   2Chronicles 28:24-25

To accomplish his mission, Hezekiah requested help from the Levites:

2Chronicles 29:5-7: *Hear me, Levites! Now sanctify yourselves, sanctify the house of the Lord God of your fathers, and carry out the rubbish from the holy place. For our fathers have trespassed and done evil in the eyes of the Lord our God; they have forsaken Him, have turned their faces away from the dwelling place of the Lord, and turned their backs on Him. They have also shut up the doors of the vestibule, put out the lamps, and have not burned incense or offered burnt offerings in the holy place to the God of Israel.*

God's people were cut off from God. The lamps were put out, and spiritual darkness prevailed in Israel. To break the power of darkness over the people of Judah, the king knew he had to repair the temple. After much cleansing was completed and the worship ministry started again, a remarkable thing happened.

2Chronicles 29:27: *Then Hezekiah commanded them to offer the burnt offering on the altar. And when the burnt offering began, the song of the Lord also began, with the trumpets and with the instruments of David king of Israel.*

The song of the Lord is not merely a random song sung unto God, but it is His song sung from within us. It proclaimed that His presence was restored to Jerusalem!

In the same way, the song of the Lord in our lives, our inner temples, is being released when Christ is formed in us, and rules in us.

Ephesians 2:10: *For we are His workmanship, created in Christ Jesus for good works, which God prepared beforehand that we should walk in them.*

'Workmanship' in Greek implies a song, or a poem. Our lives should be a song heard by others, a poem to inspire others, to attract many to acknowledge the King. Once every member of my inner temple is filled with His presence, the song within me will rise like a full orchestra directed by the Maestro – for His glory to be proclaimed in heaven and on earth. Ministry and life will then sound forth as a song. Those in the spiritual realm will hear our lives as a sweet song about Jesus, a testimony of His redemption. The melody of my life goes outwardly to proclaim His Lordship, to reach the world in a very effective way.

Features of our Inner Temples

A saying from Saint Sophrony (1896-1993) from the monastery of St. John the Baptist, UK:

It is impossible to live the Christian life.
The only thing we can do is to die daily.

The daily dying of self unites us with the Crucified Jesus. When the Lord finds such surrender[226] and longing for His complete salvation to be worked out in our lives, persistence in prayer and humility, then He may even grant us the honour to enter into paths of shame and disgrace, to be united with Him in His suffering.[227] This will be counted as grace to us, to break the fleshly hold on the self, and put the old man in us to death, for the power of resurrection to be released in us. This is the only way for the Beatitudes to become an established reality in us.[228]

---

226. Luke 22:24
227. 1Peter 4:13; Romans 8:17
228. Romans 14:8; Matthew 10:39

There can never be a higher calling, but to host the King of kings in His fullness within us; the Crucified One, the Resurrected One, the Glorified One![229]

The following characteristics are pre-requisites for the temple of God. None of the following features stand separate from the others, neither do any have lesser value than the others. Rather, together they form the fragrance of Christ in our lives. We cannot reach any of it outside of Christ. It is His sanctifying Presence in us, through the work of His gracious Holy Spirit, who transforms our old man into a holy place, consecrated unto God.

✝ **A consecrated life** is declared sacred unto God alone. My life no longer belongs to me, or to the world. We lose ourselves for His sake. There is no room for any foreign gods in my life.
Matthew 16:24-25: *Jesus said to His disciples, 'If anyone wants to come after Me, let him deny himself, and take up his cross, and be following Me. For whoever wants to save his life will lose it. But whoever loses his life for My sake will find it.'*

✝ To host the Holy One, our lives should be **Pure** and **Holy**. God said to Moses that *'no one can see Me and live,'*[230] whereas, in the New Testament, Jesus said, *'Blessed are the pure in heart for they shall see God.'*[231] Holiness is the solution for this ancient dichotomy.[232] Absence of sin is only the preparation for deep purging, the creation of a consecrated heart!
2Corinthians 7:1: *Therefore, having these promises, beloved, let us cleanse ourselves from all filthiness of the flesh and*

---

229. Ephesians 2:22; John 14:23
230. Exodus 33:20
231. Matthew 5:8
232. 2Corinthians 6:14 - 7:1

spirit, perfecting holiness in the fear of God.
1Peter 1:16: *Be holy for I am holy.*
The longer passage is beautifully practical – vv. 12-17.

✝ A Consecrated Life is established through regular **Confession and Repentance.** Confession is at the heart of our Christian walk, to stand in His light, in His grace and compassion, and acknowledge our short comings, our weaknesses, and our sins. We should not associate repentance with a negative feeling, a feeling of condemnation, as we come to realise how much we fall short of His glory. In fact, repentance cancels out all condemnation from the enemy, and from people. Repentance enables us, through the powerful blood of Jesus, to be changed into the newness of the last Adam. Repentance enables us to stop walking in the flesh, and instead to walk in the Spirit.[233] Repentance brings about forgiveness.[234] It cancels judgment. Repentance is the vehicle to being beautified, the door to complete transformation and glory.
Hebrews 12:1ᵇ: *Let us lay aside every weight, and the sin which so easily ensnares us, and let us run with endurance the race that is set before us.*

✝ To host our King, we should love His **Word.** Each Word of God is alive, breathed out by God Himself,[235] written under the inspiration of the Holy Spirit. The Word of God holds the commandments of God, the mysteries of God, the promises of God. Jesus is the living Word[236], and we want to eat the Word to shape and form our inner lives with Life and Everlasting truth.[237] Each word

---

233. Galatians 5:16,25
234. 1John 1:9
235. 2Timothy 3:16-17
236. John 1:1-2
237. Jeremiah 15:16

has a specific purpose and place in our lives and carries salvation power to realign us, awaken us, and prepare us to be united with God. Each word demands obedience. We should yield to the greatness of eternity living within each word. Each instruction is given for our benefit, to taste true freedom, true peace, perfect love from within the Trinity.

Colossians 3:16: *Let the Word of Christ dwell in you richly, teaching and admonishing one another in all wisdom, singing psalms and hymns and spiritual songs, with thankfulness in your hearts to God.*

† We should **Obey** His commandments. Obedience is the hearkening of a higher authority.
Luke 11:28: *Blessed rather are those who hear the Word of God and keep it!*
John 14:15: *If you love Me, you will keep My commandments.*[238]

† Jesus is humble, and requires **Meekness** and **Poverty of spirit.**[239] He could never find His rest in the midst of superiority and self-importance.
Matthew 11:29ᵃ: *Learn from Me, for I am gentle and lowly in heart.*

A contrite heart is considered to be a second heaven.
Isaiah 57:15: *I dwell in the high and holy place, and with him who has a contrite and humble spirit, to revive the spirit of the humble, and to revive the heart of the contrite ones.*

† We should be continuously filled with the **Holy Spirit,**[240] to be strengthened by His power in every work.

---

238. Also 1John 5:2
239. Matthew 5:5,3
240. John 3:34

Ephesians 5:18: *Do not get drunk with wine, for that is debauchery, but be filled with the Spirit.*

The true temple that hosts the King, always has the freshness of a daily infilling from the River of Life, to wash and refresh us, and society at large. We live in a very dry generation, a spiritual drought, in a society that has never tasted any pure water.[241] We do not even know spiritual purity ourselves, as so much is mixed and convoluted. Oh, how society would respond to pure, spiritual water! This river flows from God's throne,[242] bringing forth fruits, and healing of nations.[243]

✝ A true temple carries a **Responsibility for our Generation,** even with tears. God cannot dwell in hearts that are self-focussed and self-absorbed. God has special ways to reach the hearts of those on our streets, in our shopping malls, and in the sport arenas. No method of evangelism or missiological strategy can reach this generation. We need to receive from God a burden and an anointing to love and serve all.

Matthew 9:36: *When He saw the crowds, He had compassion for them, because they were harassed and helpless, like sheep without a shepherd.*

✝ Each individual temple is alive with **Bridal love** for the coming Bridegroom. There is deep longing for the return of the King, the Second Coming.[244]

We are familiar with different kinds of love: the love of the Father, brotherly love, friendship, compassion etc. However, bridal love is distinct in its purity and power. It is the brilliance of the light shining from Zion.

---

241. Jeremiah 9:11-12
242. Ezekiel 47:1-5
243. Ezekiel 47:12; Revelation 22:1,2
244. Matthew 25 – Parable of the 10 virgins

Pure, bridal love draws the King near, and brings great pleasure to Him.

† A true disciple of Jesus lives an **Orderly and Disciplined life**, a life where priorities are clearly defined. We strive to establish daily structures for prayer and the Word, in building unseen altars in our homes and families. Our weekly schedule includes regular fasting, and the Sabbath is set apart unto the Lord. We schedule our year, month by month, to consecrate the holy days unto Him.

1Corinthians 9:24-27: *Do you not know that in a race all the runners run, but only one receives the prize? So run that you may obtain it. Every athlete exercises self-control in all things. They do it to receive a perishable wreath, but we an imperishable. So I do not run aimlessly; I do not box as one beating the air. But I discipline my body and keep it under control, lest after preaching to others I myself should be disqualified.*

Many features still remain to be mentioned:

† Each individual temple is filled with **light**, and lives in the *fellowship of Light*.[245]

John 12:36: *While you have the light, believe in the light, that you may become sons of light.*

Moses reflected the light from the outside, but we are to radiate the indwelling Christ from within.

Matthew 5:14,16: *You are the light of the world. A city that is set on a hill cannot be hidden. Let your light so shine before men, that they may see your good works, and glorify your Father in heaven.*

† Each temple is filled with **faith**.[246] Faith is an energy, the fuel that propels our walk forward.

---

245.   1John 1:17
246.   Ephesians 3:12; Hebrews 11:6

† Each temple is filled with **discernment**, the constant **renewal of the mind**.[247] Sadly, arrogance and falsehood is the currency of this generation.

† Each temple is constantly being trained in the path of **patience** and **perseverance**.[248]

† Each temple has a **childlike** spirit. Through the redeeming work of the Holy Spirit, man is restored to his original nature before the Fall, which is characterized by simplicity, transparency and inherent cheerfulness.

The Apostle Paul's life and writings are for us a model of Christ dwelling in a human being, a true Zion. He wrote to the churches in Asia Minor, to train, teach and disciple us to walk in the full measure of becoming a temple for His Presence. I conclude with a quotation from the epistle to the Philippians:

Indeed, I count everything as loss because of
the surpassing worth of knowing Christ Jesus my Lord.
For His sake I have suffered the loss of
all things and count them as rubbish,
in order that I may gain Christ and be found in Him,
not having a righteousness of my own that comes from the law,
but that which comes through faith in Christ,
the righteousness from God that depends on faith,
that I may know Him and the power of His resurrection,
and may share His sufferings, becoming like Him in His death,
that by any means possible I may attain the resurrection from the dead.

Philippians 3:8-11

---

247. 1Corinthians 2:16; 4:6
248. Luke 8:15; Galatians 5:22 23

Practical Steps

Ministering to the Lord

The four living creatures ... day and night they never cease to say,
'Holy, holy, holy, is the Lord God Almighty,
who was and is and is to come!'
And whenever the living creatures give glory and honour and thanks
to Him who is seated on the throne, who lives forever and ever,
the twenty-four elders fall down before
Him who is seated on the throne
and worship Him who lives forever and ever.
They cast their crowns before the throne, saying,
'Worthy are you, our Lord and God,
to receive glory and honour and power,
for you created all things, and by your will
they existed and were created.'

Revelation 4:8-11

If God is Who He Says He is

Allow me to tell you a story of a young man; I'll call him Pete. Pete grew up in a modern, European family of naturalists, musicians and atheists. God was not acknowledged in his upbringing. They were smart, creative, and free. Pete met God in an inexplicable encounter which suddenly redirected his life. As he knew nothing about God, the Bible, or Christianity, he immersed himself in newly found Christian friends. And he asked many questions. He did not know the difference between Moses and Paul, or Peter and Joseph. He did not know the difference between Catholics and Charismatics. He was like a child – he watched all and everybody, listening with a hungry heart. He really wanted to be a good Christian, after all Jesus encountered him with such humble light.

I met Pete roughly a year after his conversion experience. He came to me during a tea break on Monday morning after my first lecture: 'Can I please speak to you?' He then asked me a question that still makes me tremble: 'Ina, if God is who He says He is, why is it that Christians don't worship Him more?'

This question cuts through the worship practices we have adopted in modern-day Christianity where Jesus is not central, neither is He exalted. And yet, we talk as if He is worthy at all times. Jesus has become one of many components in the Christian pic-a-mix. Although we all value Him immensely, He is not necessarily, without question, the first and foremost in everything. How can we busy ourselves with Prayer and Mercy Ministries, Counselling and Deliverance, Strategies and Evangelism, and yet give little undistracted time to Him?

I have been part of intercessory groups for the past 30 years, and have attended numerous prayer meetings, conferences, nights of prayer etc. in many nations. I have seen powerful prayer, tears, and many prophetic proclamations. And as the years passed, I have been amazed at the little real changes in society.

The church, also in our generation, is praying, and is praying sacrificially. Prayer meetings are corporate, public, on Zoom, and on WhatsApp. There are weekly meetings, monthly meetings, annual conferences etc. longing for salvation and righteousness in our nations. There are contemplative prayer classes, and prophetic training courses. Intercession schools were birthed in many denominations. Prayer bulletins are circulated in every possible way. Prophetic messages are forwarded. Yet, something does not add up.

In doing some basic reading, we discover that we suffer from worse statistics in nearly every sphere of society: increase in knife crime and murders on our streets, increase in drug-use and gangs, increase in depression and suicide, increase in euthanasia, increase in human trafficking and sex slavery, increase in zero-hour contracts and poverty, increase in abortion rates, increase in divorce rates, increase in injustice and corruption of elected governments and police departments, increase in mental health decline and gender confusion, and the list goes on and on and on. Displaced peoples and refugees in many nations have more than doubled in the nations due to war, injustice, corruption, and natural disasters.

How is it possible that so many prayer movements and organisations, even stadiums filled with praying people, have not brought about from heaven the release to stop us all in our tracks?

Since the first global, corporate prayer calls came about in the world, and I think back to the call to prayer for the 10/40 Window[249] back in the 80's, society at large has become more fragmented, more aggressive and dangerous, and the church has split into smaller fragments of opinion, theology, preference and offence. I do not disregard the salvation of thousands, especially those from Unreached People Groups and Islamic nations. But society has not changed for the better. We do not experience humility, righteousness and justice in the nations. Truth has less value than ever before.

The Gospel of Mark describes the ministry of John the Baptist in that ALL in Judea and ALL in Jerusalem were baptised in repentance and confession of sins.

Mark 1:5: *All the country of Judea and all Jerusalem were going out to Him and were being baptized by Him in the river Jordan, confessing their sins.*

These crowds did not go for healing, or for miraculous multiplication of bread and fish. They went, the whole city, to repent of their sins. There was a change in the heart of society. A force from heaven enlightened their darkened hearts, and they turned from their known ways. We find another example in **Acts 13:44:** *On the coming Sabbath day almost all the city came together to hear the Word of God.*

Testimonies about answers to prayer are often about individual releases, e.g. how God supernaturally provided money to buy a necessary computer. Or healed my dad. We are always grateful and surprised when God graciously shows us that He cares, especially in the details of our little lives. But the church should not be satisfied with personal blessings, although we are grateful. Our mandate is to

---

249. www.joshuaproject.net/resources/articles/10_40_window

establish His Kingdom on earth, for the knowledge of the glory of the Lord to cover the earth as the waters cover the sea![250]

I ask forgiveness for being harsh. But it is clear to me that the emperor has no clothes on. We need to honestly consider the hard facts. We should lift our eyes to what God has in store for us.[251] What should we learn from previous generations when the Church powerfully influenced empires, brought paganism to a fall, and saw righteousness established in society? I am personally convinced that we got lost, that we somehow started to believe that God exists to bless us, my calling, my family, and my nation. This is an immense sadness. The truth is that I was created for Him, for His glory and pleasure. My life, my time and my prayers belong to Him.

Matthew 10:39: *Whoever finds his life will lose it, and whoever loses his life for My sake will find it.*

In this chapter, we will look at an ancient topic – how to practically minister to the Great and Eternal King. This aspect of eternal life is nearly completely absent in our modern Church practices. I trust the Holy Spirit to start a stirring in us, to train us to stand before Him.

Approaching the King

God is the Holy, Eternal King, and to Him belongs due respect. In ages past, different tribes had their detailed protocol on how to enter into their king's presence. To this day, the English women curtsy to King Charles III, while

---

250.   Habakkuk 2:14
251.   Isaiah 55:8-9

the men accordingly bow their heads. The Japanese and Taiwanese go lower even. In bygone ages, African kings expected their subjects to crawl on their stomachs in his presence. Refusing regal protocol, or even neglecting it in ignorance, could cost you your life. Well, at least in times gone by.

The King of kings surpasses any earthly king. His Kingdom is exalted, an everlasting Kingdom. How do we enter into His presence? There are immediate verses that come to mind, and you are probably already quoting these.

Hebrews 10:19-22: *Therefore, brothers, having boldness to enter into the Holy of Holies by the blood of Jesus, by a new and living way which He has consecrated for us through the veil, that is to say, His flesh; and having a High Priest over the house of God, let us draw near with a true heart in full assurance of faith, having our hearts sprinkled from an evil conscience and our bodies having been washed with pure water.*

You may argue that the way to God was opened for us by the blood of Jesus through His crucifixion and resurrection. There is therefore no restriction on my behaviour in the Heavenly Throne Room, you may say. He is my Father! I am His child! Therefore, we draw near with candid boldness.

Hebrews 4:16ª: *Let us then approach God's throne of grace with confidence.*

Yes, we are grateful to God for Jesus, for shedding His precious blood in opening for us the living way to the Father. Yet, we cannot assume a casualness. While being spiritual children, there is grace and time to learn the eternal ways of God. But as we mature in Christ, as we grow in understanding of our responsibility for His

Kingdom in our nations, we should progress in heavenly behaviour. To worship as a priest in the Holy Place as is expected of us, we should follow the heavenly protocol according to God's eternal ways. We should unlearn some of our childish habits, and allow our inner spirit-man to be taught to address the King Eternal in everlasting ways. Divine history will not give post-moderns and millennials a free pass. Our generation needs to humble itself in the light of the Greatness of the Eternal One, to whom all angels, living creatures and saints bow low.

It is impossible to minister to God from a distance. So how do we draw near God, in order to stand before Him as a priest?

Heavenly Protocol

Deep humility and detailed preparation were required from the High Priest to go behind the veil in the temple, once a year on the Day of Atonement.[252] Imminent death was a reality for a human being stepping into the Holy Place, even though the mercy seat was covering the law. Neither can we rush into God's presence and demand answers to our prayers and crisis. We can learn from queen Esther as she approached king Ahasuerus with careful preparations and trepidation, knowing that she was overstepping palatial protocol. And yet, she carried the future of her people, the people of God, as her responsibility.[253] This was not the time to be free-spirited and individualistic. She carefully submitted in great humility, and overturned history. If she had acted in false confidence, the outcome of history may have looked very different.

---

252.   Leviticus 16
253.   Esther 5:1-2

The Ministry of Angels

YHWH is a God of order. Coming before His throne is to stand on eternal ground, and the protocols to be followed are beyond time, both for angelic beings and humans, for those who departed this life, and those alive on earth.

We can learn from the angels about how to approach the King. The angels have not only ministered to God through all ages, but they minister directly in His presence. They have never sinned. What they do seems overly simplistic, yet always with pure, burning hearts. They repeat mostly one prayer while bowing down in His presence: Holy, holy, holy! This sounds very simple, and yet it contains a mystery. In the book of Isaiah we read, as the prophet is allowed to witness the worship of the seraphim, that they cover their eyes and their feet, and only fly with two wings, although they each has six wings.

Isaiah 6:1-3: *In the year that King Uzziah died I saw the Lord sitting upon a throne, high and lifted up; and the train of his robe filled the temple. Above Him stood the seraphim. Each had six wings: with two he covered his face, and with two he covered his feet, and with two he flew. One called to another and said: 'Holy, holy, holy is the LORD of hosts; the whole earth is full of His glory!'*

This is the impact that the presence of the Eternal One has on these glorious, sinless creatures. They were deeply humbled, even filled with fear, and did not show their own glory in His presence, but rather covered their faces and feet. How much more should we, redeemed sinners, pursue and continue to practice ancient, holy ways in approaching the holy Triune God!

In the book of Hebrews, we learn how the angels minister to God:

Hebrews 1:14: *Are they not all ministering spirits [liturgia] sent out to serve [diakonea] for the sake of those who are to inherit salvation?*

Angels have an all-consuming God-focus, and sometimes an earthly responsibility at God's command. They minister to God in the heavenlies, and they also serve people on earth in obedience to God's commands.

When angels are sent to minister to people on earth (*diakonea)*, they intervene in specific earthly circumstances, or deliver divine messages. Angels can carry warnings, explanations, instructions, encouragements, enlightening words etc. These messages are always changing, always freshly inspired by God Himself. The message the angel brought to Joseph[254], the betrothed of Mary, is different from the message he brought to apostle Peter in prison.[255] *Diakonea* is always changing, unique to each situation.

The word *liturgia* suggests repetition. As we come into the Holy of Holies where He is eternally enthroned above the cherubim, we find that prayer is simple, directed at Him only. And it is precise.

Humans were created, just like the angels, to function in both realms. We are seated on thrones in the heavenlies,[256] and we are given authority on earth to establish His Kingdom. We can enter into the heavenlies with worship and adoration – with *liturgia* - to minister to God. We no

---

254. Matthew 1:20-21
255. Acts 12:5-17
256. Ephesians 2:6

longer worship from the bottom of the mountain, or before the veil. We are allowed to actually enter the Holy Place.[257]

Ministering to God was one of the main components that enriched and marked the spirituality of the early Church. In the New Testament, we read how the apostles ministered in transforming pagan Asia Minor:

Acts 13:2: *As they ministered to the Lord and fasted, the Holy Spirit said, So then, separate Barnabas and Saul to Me for the work to which I have called them.*

This took place roughly twelve years after Jesus' death and resurrection. The disciples were gathered together to minister to God (*liturgia*), standing before Him as priests in their generation. They were not having a time of worship and intercession – as we would read it today with our modern glasses. They were ministering unto the Lord, bringing ancient prayers repetitively before Him with hearts that were deeply concerned for their generation. We find that God responded in this humble moment by giving them missiological instructions about their responsibility to Gentile nations, as the first apostles were sent to nations beyond Jewish boundaries. The horizontal release was birthed in a vertical stance before God. And it was accompanied with anointing to fulfil God's purposes.

The flow from heaven into the nations is immeasurable if we submit to eternal ways in approaching the King.

---

257.   Hebrews 10:19

Liturgia

The word *liturgia* has over time come to be translated as 'serving', or 'worshipping', with increasingly free interpretation of the application thereof. As time passed, the practice of liturgy and repetitive prayers has sadly become a stale recurrence of religious words, and has been nearly completely stolen from many denominations and church traditions. Offering the same words over and over again to God is culturally strange to a generation of evangelical believers. We find it monotonous, restrictive, even legalistic. It is not uncommon for the practice of liturgy to be dismissed. It has little value for many. Eastern Church traditions value liturgy, but often the heavenly dimension is assumed, and not experienced. In such cases, even the ancient, holy practice of liturgy becomes earthly, with little connection to the heavenly realm, and little impact on society.

To worship means something different to each one of us today. We offer free, personalised prayers unto the Lord; songs, music and joyful gratitude, oftentimes shaped by the spirit of the world and generational preferences. A mega barrier to overcome is to realise that worship does not belong to me. The purpose of worship is not to bring me comfort, or to express myself in sadness, joy, or even faith. Worship belongs to Him, to please Him only.

If I could draw a simple diagram to explain this, then I would draw worship as an arrow pointing towards God. Worship is not a downwards arrow ministering to me, or even outwards to the needy world. And yet, in pure worship we will always find that He responds. He comforts and gives us instructions, and revelations. He encourages, and strengthens. As we bring to Him our trust and love, He pours into us from heaven, uniting us in Him. And yet, we never enter into worship with the purpose of being blessed. My only objective is to minister to Him. If He does touch me, it is pure grace! If He does not, then I am still richer for bringing my worship to Him.

God is deeply interested in the state of our hearts. Bringing many words to Him is confusing, so to speak - He does not like noise. If we can bring Him only one word from a pure heart, it will please Him, and He will act on our behalf beyond our imagination. When we approach Him with a humble spirit, while bowing to His Lordship, our prayers may bear everlasting results on earth.

Any intercessor will be limited in his/her prayer life until we learn how to minister to God. *Liturgia* is the protocol that bring us into the King's presence. It prepares our hearts to unite with Him, to bring intercession and supplications in one Spirit, to petition Him to respond to our cry.

Eternal Ways

We can learn much from the life of Jesus while He was on earth, the incarnated God-man, how He related to His Father as a human being. Jesus is our High Priest, and we should mirror Him as He goes behind the torn veil, as He stands at the heavenly altar.

Jesus was and is always concerned with only one thing – to please the Father. At the age of twelve, He was longing to stay near His Father.[258] Throughout His ministry we find Him in the early mornings, going up to lonely places, to pray.[259] Jesus was ministering to His Father in heaven –

---

258.   Luke 2:49
259.   Mark 1:35

doing *liturgia*, as He was holding the crowds in His heart with all their needs. But the Father came first. Jesus is our perfect model of having a vertical stance, resulting in a horizontal overflow of life that changed history.

Because of Jesus' sinless life He could enter the most Holy Place in His crucifixion to make atonement with His precious blood on the mercy seat in heaven, and open the way for us to the Father in His resurrection.[260] The veil tore in the temple. He conquered sin and death to open the way for us to approach God in the Most Holy Place.

Jesus is the eternal Priest. Due to a covenant sealed by His blood, we are also restored to this heavenly priesthood. We can never enter by ourselves, separate from Jesus. We are clothed with Christ if we are baptised in His death.[261] The Spirit raises us up with Him,[262] and brings us to the Father. In Christ, we have a daily priestly responsibility in the heavenlies to serve Him in the nations.

If we don't walk in this royal priesthood,[263] then our ministry on earth is greatly hindered.

The early Church did not neglect free and unstructured prayer and worship, using inspired words spontaneously. The free expression of prayer is valuable as it presents our hearts to God with prophetic inspirations and impressions for life, and for ministry. But we should not overlook the orderly protocol of entering into His presence, before we present to Him our supplications.

---

260. Hebrews 10:20
261. Romans 6:4-5
262. Romans 8:11
263. 1Peter 2:9

One of the unfortunate things of our generation which greatly influences our spiritual lives, is our lack of consistency and patient endurance. Some days we pray in a certain way, and other days we don't pray at all. Every day has its own flow and unique ways of relating to God, or not relating to Him. No two days are alike. The structure and discipline of liturgical prayer strengthens and straightens my personality to stand in heavenly places and serve faithfully on earth.

God's Delight

God created us for His pleasure:

Isaiah 43:7: *Everyone who is called by My name; for I have created him for My glory, I have formed him; yes, I have made him.*

Revelation 4:11: *O Lord, You are worthy to receive glory and honour and power, because You created all things, and for Your pleasure they existed and were created.*

God is not selfish. On the contrary, He is love,[264] and the giver of Life.[265] He longs to draw us closer to Him so that we can partake in His life, to receive from Him all the fullness He offers us. Ministering to Him is both a privilege, and a responsibility.

Proverbs 8:30b-31: *I was daily His delight, rejoicing always before Him; rejoicing in the world, His earth; and my delight was with the sons of men.*

---

264.   1John 4:16
265.   Job 33:14; Nehemiah 9:6; John 1:3-4; Psalm 36:9

Whilst on earth, the Father proclaimed from heaven: *This is my Son, in whom is my delight.*[266] Jesus pleased the Father, even to His last breath on the cross as He surrendered His spirit in perfect peace. As we follow in Jesus' footsteps, carrying our cross, we also can become God's delight. This is our deepest need, our utmost satisfaction - to enter into this mutual delight: His delights in us, and we delight in Him! When this happens, it is like a current of electricity which is released during worship and intercession. His eternal life starts to flow continuously in me. We are united for His life-giving purposes on earth in this river of mutual love.

The issue at hand is not about God loving us, but about God delighting in us. Yes, of course, we believe that God always loves everybody. He never stopped loving us, even when we were unfaithful. God always loves, and will always love. God continues to love us, even if He does not delight in us. He can have a broken heart towards me, a wounded heart because of rebellion, disobedience, and ongoing sin patterns. It saddens Him when I find my delight in other things – daily activities, possessions, relationships and success. It is dangerous to find spiritual delight in the very things He generously gifted us: ministry, spiritual gifts etc.

Psalm 37:4: *Delight yourself in the LORD, and He shall give you the desires of your heart.*

As we approach His throne, finding our delight in Him, He will extend His right arm of righteousness and power towards us and our circumstances. If we turn in our core to Him, standing before Him as priests, a stream of eternal life starts to flow, because He delights in us. And it will overflow to others. This is heaven on earth.

---

266.   Matthew 3:17; Matthew 17:5

Nothingness Before God

In the light of eternity, I am nothing. We should take a page from the books of the Church Fathers and embrace our nothingness. There is nothing good in me. I know deep within that I have nothing good in me.

Matthew 5:3: *Blessed are the poor in spirit, for theirs is the kingdom of heaven.*

Romans 7:18: *For I know that nothing good dwells in me, that is, in my flesh. For I have the desire to do what is right, but not the ability to carry it out.*

Naturally our fallen nature is desperate for vainglory, success, even in prayer. The Holy Spirit does this gentle work in our lives to reach a point of 'nothingness.' Only then can God entrust us with His glory, and there is no limit for such a person to be used by God if we become a delight unto Him, an empty channel carrying His glory.

Practical Steps

Praying the Psalms

One thing have I asked of the LORD, that will I seek after:
that I may dwell in the house of the LORD all the days of my life,
to gaze upon the beauty of the LORD
and to inquire in His temple.

Psalm 27:4

The story is told about a poor man who lived in Upper Egypt, illiterate, with only basic knowledge of farming, but he was desiring to worship God day and night in a worthy way. He left his village and journeyed to a monastery in the desert to be instructed. These monks were advanced in spiritual experiences and theology. Upon arrival, the farmer addressed a monk: 'I have a fire burning in my heart and want to pray day and night. Please teach me to pray.' The monk responded to him, 'I will teach you a short prayer. Memorize it, and repeat it often. Come back in a month and I will teach you more.' But a few hours later, the farmer returned to the monastery, having already forgotten the words of the newly taught prayer. The monk was a wise man, filled with prophetic insight, and he discerned the mystery behind this farmer. So he asked him, 'Do you have any money?' The poor man humbly exclaimed, 'Father, you know I have nothing. I came to ask you about prayer, why do you ask me about money?' The old monk was now really puzzled. He said, 'There is a river between your village and this monastery. How did you come across the river?' To this, the farmer answered shyly, 'I did not have the fare for the ferry-ride. Do you see this cloak on my shoulders? When I reached the river, I rolled it up like this, and put it on the water to open a way, and then I walked across on dry ground. This is my means of transportation.' Now the monk was really interested: 'Tell me about your prayer life. How do you usually pray?' Very embarrassed, the farmer admitted, 'I memorized the Lord's prayer when I was just a boy, but this is the only prayer I know. I repeat it day and night.' The Father blessed the poor man and sent him home to continue in what he has been doing all his life. He admitted that he could not teach him anything. The monk then told his followers the mystery of this farmer: 'This man has a pure heart and is completely filled with the Holy Spirit. He lives in the realm of miracles and wonders. He has used only one prayer every day, all his life. Here we use all kinds of prayers, but have never reached such a degree of infilling with the Person of the Holy Spirit, such oneness with God.'

This story from the fifth century is an example of how much God is interested in the condition of our hearts in prayer, rather than an impressive flow of spiritual phrases. God is not moved by complex prayers. He longs for us to be restored to a simple and direct dialogue with Him, without shame, or pretence. In recent times we emphasise the role of the intellect and logic in prayer. We have been estranged from innocent, pure hearts lifted to God in childlikeness, even silence before His throne.

Matthew 5:5: *Blessed are the meek! For they shall inherit the earth.*

God intervenes on earth because of His grace, not because of our impressive prayers. If prayer is according to His heart's desire, then His arm is always released.

Over the past twenty years I have had the privilege to be part of a Christian group embracing and practicing the worship model of the early Apostolic Church from the first four centuries. I was able to attend lectures, listen to conversations, and ask questions; but more important than anything, I have been allowed to worship with them these many years. If I have to be honest about this experience, then I would admit that it often felt like David wearing the battle attire of Saul.[267] Too big. Too Hard. Too inflexible. Too Uncomfortable. And simply not for me. I couldn't move in it. I couldn't find myself in it. And I couldn't face the world in it. It belonged to yesterday generations.

Gradually, over years, I started to understand that something was happening within me that is not easily pin-pointed in words. There was a steady change, a humbling, an opening up of my heart. And as the years passed, and I continued to

---

267.   1Samuel 17:38

join them in these ancient prayers, I realised that my view of God, my experience of the Eternal One, was different from my other Christian friends. God became bigger. More present. More awesome.

Worshipping with the Psalms became prayer for me. When I was worried about my siblings, or stressed by the environmental ruin, or when I was simply emotional and lonely, I turned to the Psalms. Praying the Psalms lifts my gaze, and secures my feet on solid ground. Psalms connects me with generations past who prayed the exact same prayers; and with the heavens, as they are ministering to God right now in everlasting ways. I no longer had to try and find words for things that were beyond me. I could simply stand, and be embraced by the ongoing, eternal worship of heaven.

The Early Apostolic Church

Praying and worshipping with the Psalms daily has a magnificent history. The first Christian groups did not set themselves apart from existing Jewish worship, but they would go daily up to the Temple for prayer. It was never God's intention to separation the Church from the Jews – rather a smooth unfolding from the Old into the New. The new-born Church continued to pray in the ancient ways of Israel. They prayed the Psalms as the nation of Israel did for many generations, since the time Moses established the tabernacle. David wrote many of the Psalms in his lifetime, and it belonged to the worship pattern of the temple in Zion. Throughout the ages the Jews followed certain set hours for prayer in the temple. They would gather to pray and/ or sing the psalms with expectation, awaiting the Messiah. They used to have choirs, accompanied by sacred musical instruments. One group would chant a verse(s), and the other would respond antiphonically.

The importance of the Old Testament can often be minimalised, considered as fulfilled in Christ. However, the Early Church believed that the Old Testament holds God's eternal thoughts and ways for His people. God's mind does not change. We should look at the Old Testament through the eyes of the New Testament. While we no longer live under the law, worship did not change.

Jesus would have prayed the Psalms throughout His life, and also with His disciples. The new believers, the Church-just-born, understood that worship unto God is ongoing and eternal, even as they stepped across the threshold into a new dispensation. There was no need to throw out the old, and create a new set of worship. In the New Testament the apostles continued in the same external structure, though with new hearts. In **Acts 3:1** the Apostles Peter and John went up to the temple at the ninth hour, about 3pm. In **Acts 10:9** Apostle Peter went up on the housetop to pray at the sixth hour – which is midday.

The use of Scripture was absolutely central to the Early Church. The way they would worship with the prophetic books was different to the way that they would read the historical books. It was also different from the way they looked at the Gospels, or the epistles of Paul and the other apostles. They considered the Scriptures as worship, not as study material to increase knowledge. They would use opening phrases and concluding phrases to each book of Scripture, each book different from the next, to unlock living worship. For example, when the early Fathers prayed the Psalms, they concluded each Psalm with the word *'Alleluia'*, chanting it with a melody. The book of Psalms was seen as the Book of Worship, inspired by the Holy Spirit to be prayed before God at all times.

However, when they prayed the Gospels, they made a prostration at the end of each chapter with the phrase *'Glory be to God,'* acknowledging our need of a Saviour who enables us to walk in the fullness of Truth. On the other hand, when they worshiped with the epistles, they concluded with *'May the grace of God the Father be with us,'* to remind themselves that the epistles are rooted in grace.

Even though we long to worship from our spirit, oftentimes our worship is a mixture from our minds, emotions and spirits. The Early Church was zealous in discerning between pure worship coming from our spirits, and soulish worship. To purify our worship unto God, our spirits need to feed regularly on special food to strengthen, mature and activate it, so that worship will flow in purity and harmony with eternity. Praying the Psalms presents divine incense to Him who is worthy, in continuation with the past 5000+ years.

If we surrender our time and words to Him, lifting eager hearts to Him, then praying the Psalms daily will humble us, lift us into heavenly realms, and will unite us with the Church throughout the ages, to pray with one voice, in one Spirit.

Spontaneous Prayer

Traditionally, the Church Fathers followed a divine order in prayer. They began with Psalm-prayer to strengthen their spirits, and to gather their scattered thoughts. Psalm-prayer was the preparation to enter into spontaneous prayers and free conversation with God. This was called *'praying with unveiled faces.'*[268]

---

268.   2Corinthians 3:18

However, as the Bible teaches us, and as we also know from experience, the actual truth is that *'we do not know what we should pray for as we ought.'* However, God's word promises us that *'the Spirit helps in our weaknesses'*, and that the Spirit Himself *'makes intercession for us with groanings which cannot be uttered.'*[269] For the Spirit to freely intercede inside us, for His inspiration to lead us in free dialogue with God, we first have to shake off anything that has clung to us from the world in which we live. Also, the activity of the flesh in us should be reigned in; this includes the dominance of the mind, thoughts, and the desires of the soul. Psalm-prayer lifts our hearts, guides us into His presence, and releases our inner beings to pray prayers beyond our own understanding. But this cannot happen unless our spirits are regularly strengthened and nurtured through the Psalms.

Undeniably, Psalm-prayer is considered as the preparation for prayer so that the work of the Holy Spirit is fully released in us.

Praying the Agpia

Praying the Psalms was normal during the first centuries, and different structures were developed to help believers to pray the Psalms. A more advanced and mature group of worshippers lived in the area of Wadi El Natroun in northern Egypt. These men and women used to pray all hundred and fifty Psalms each day. These worshippers grew to become unrestricted and spacious in their spirits, and were able to spend days in continuous prayer, as much in the heavenlies as on earth. This group prayed all day, as Christ said in **Luke 18:1:** *That men always ought to pray and not lose heart.*

---

269.   Romans 8:26

This statement was repeated through the ages.[270]

Another group of worshippers, living in the southern part of Egypt, were beginners in their faith. The Agpia,[271] or also known as **The Short Psalms** was specifically prepared for these beginners, enabling them to pray selected Psalms daily at different hours. The Agpia is divided into seven blocks of prayer, in accordance with **Psalm 119:164:** *Seven times a day I praise you.*

Each block of prayer in the Agpia contains twelve chosen Psalms related to a particular salvific event in the life of Christ, although the reference of each Psalm is not always direct.

✝ For example, at six o'clock in the morning, which is the **First Hour** of prayer, the psalms prayed are about the resurrection of Christ, as He rose early in the morning.[272]

✝ At the **Third Hour** of prayer, which is nine o'clock, the focus is on the outpouring of the Holy Spirit according to **Acts chapter two**. Alongside the twelve chosen Psalms, a passage of the Gospel of John is prayed, highlighting the coming of the Holy Spirit.

✝ At the **Sixth Hour** of prayer, at midday, the focus of prayer is the Crucifixion of Christ. At this hour we read the Beatitudes to remind us that we could never reach these principles; unless we die with Christ.

---

270.   1Thessalonians 5:17; Ephesians 6:18; Philippians 4:6; Luke 18:1; Psalm 86:3, 116:2

271.   Also spelled *Agpeya*. The **Agpia** is a Coptic Orthodox Prayer Book – '*the book of hours.*' It was inspired by the desert fathers in the 5th century, and contains prayers for seven different set times throughout the day. The hours are chronological, each corresponding to events in the life of our Lord Jesus Christ. These set prayers are easily found on the Internet, or on multiple apps on smart phones. It is also available in Coptic Book stores.

272.   Luke 24:1-2

✝ At three o'clock in the afternoon, the **Ninth Hour** of prayer focusses on Jesus breathing out His last breath on the cross. The chosen Psalms are songs of worship, for our joy is completed, our salvation is sealed. *It is finished!* [273]

✝ At five o'clock in the afternoon we prayer the **Sunset Prayer**, at the time when the body of Jesus Christ was taken down from the cross, and was prepared for burial. These are delicate moments when a few people had the honour to wash and minister to His broken body, and lay His lifeless body to rest.

✝ At six o'clock in the evening the day ends, and in praying the **Twelve Hour** we are reminded that our life could end any minute. We don't like to think about our own death, but we are only temporarily on earth.

✝ The last hour of prayer each day is at **Midnight**. We eagerly expect the Second Coming of our Lord and King, awaiting Him as our Bridegroom at midnight.[274] It is a bridal hour, and the atmosphere is filled with anticipation and love. We pray Psalm 119 in renewing our covenant with God. In praying this particular Psalm regularly, we experience restoration in our desire for prayer, energising our spirits from within.

Praying the Psalms fills us with an anointing of worship, as seen in David, as his appetite for, and focus in worship increased throughout his life.

Psalm 27:4: *One thing have I asked of the LORD, that will I seek after: that I may dwell in the house of the LORD all the days of*

---

273. John 19:30
274. Matthew 25

my life, to gaze upon the beauty of the LORD and to inquire in His temple.

As we pray the twelve Psalms and the Gospel passages in each of the assigned hours, we find within our hearts a great need for God's mercy. At this point in the Agpia prayer, for nearly two millennia already, worshippers would repeat *Lord, have mercy* forty-one times. The number forty-one speaks of the passion of Christ: thirty-nine lashes of the whip, the nails, and the sword piercing His side. By praying these prayers of mercy, we acknowledged that the suffering of Christ has become the source of our salvation and strength, and we drink deep from His well of salvation.

Prostrations

After each Psalm, they would bow in prostrating themselves before God, touching the ground with their foreheads, before getting up to stand before Him again. Prostration has a comprehensive meaning, to the extent that the early Church considered it as a type of worship in itself. They could make multiple prostrations before the Lord uttering very few words.

In the book of Revelation, we get to peek through a small window into the heavenly pattern of worship. The way of worship in the book of Revelation can be summed up in two words: Praise. And Prostrations.

Revelation 7:11: *All the angels stood around the throne, and the elders, and the four living creatures, and they fell before the throne on their faces and worshiped God.*

Revelation 11:16: *The twenty-four elders sitting before God on their thrones, fell on their faces and worshiped God.*

All the heavenly orders, archangels, cherubim and seraphim, living creatures, saints and the departed, continue to worship the Lord in bowing before Him. To no surprise the Early Fathers believed that prostrating themselves before the Lord is one method of worship that will continue into all eternity, and that we should practice it here on earth: **Matthew 6:10:** *On earth as it is in heaven.*

The fruit following the act of bowing is multi-faceted. **Romans 12:1** calls us to *'offer our bodies as living sacrifices … this is our spiritual act of worship.'* Our earthly bodies can participate in worship with our spirits and minds. When the body participates in worship, it is being sanctified, and its natural instincts and desires are disciplined.

The Greek word for worship, *proskuneō* [275] literally means to crawl on the floor on all fours, to enter into the presence of one greater than I. *Proskuneō* describes worship as giving respect and gratitude in a clear act of humility and love. Often, as we physically go low before God, we will experience a spontaneous flow of words of love welling up deep from within. At other times, repentance and prayers of humility are expressed.

† In bowing before God, we proclaim His Lordship in our lives that breaks all other authorities. For many generations the practice of prostration was a method used in self-deliverance from demonic forces, as well as to break the bondages of persistent sins.

† In prostrating, we become partakers with Christ in His death, making a proclamation in the Spirit that we have also died to sin. Yet, we are raised with Jesus Christ in resurrection.

---

275.   Strong's dictionary: **G4352**

- As we move downwards, we are symbolically entering into the grave.
- As we get up, we are being raised into resurrection life.

In prostrating daily before God, we are asking for the power of Christ's resurrection to raise us into new dimensions of life.[276] We cannot experience this grace, unless we practice it regularly.

† Bowing restores unity and harmony between the different disconnected aspects and members in our lives. In creation, mankind was in harmony within ourselves – a whole unit, filled with his Spirit. Yet, in the Fall the members of our lives became fragmented, separated and broken. The mind, soul and body became disconnected from each other, even warring with each other. Prostrating before God increases the process of integration and restoration, to become whole again.

† As we regularly bow before God, a spiritual shield is being established around our physical bodies which protects us from demonic temptations and influences. Repeated bowing for longer periods of time, will create a safe place for us where His presence dwells within and around us.

To conclude this short introduction on praying the Psalms, just a few last thoughts.

The Psalms have an amazing mystery as a **Book of Prayer**. It is considered spiritual food, the New Testament manna for the spirit which, when prayed regularly, have definitive results in the formation and nourishing of our inner spirit-man. God fed Israel in the desert every day the same food

---

276   Philippians 3:10

– manna - for forty years. He never changed the menu, because He was forming the heart and spirit of a new nation, laying the foundation of the identity of a nation with a specific calling to represent Him on earth to all other nations.

This food is mystical, to nourish spiritual infants and the spiritually advanced at the same time. The Psalms feed spiritual babies and toddlers as pure spiritual milk,[277] and it can be solid food suitable for the spiritually mature.[278] This is because the Holy Spirit, the author of the book of Psalms, is the One who prays these Psalms in us, and opens their treasures inside the human soul, according to the spiritual stature of each person. Therefore, spiritual infants drinking this spiritual Psalm milk may experience spiritual comfort, joy and an inner fervency, sometimes with spiritual tears. Psalm prayer becomes a place of belonging, as if we are embraced, held. This continues throughout the stages of spiritual infancy and childhood.

Once we mature into spiritual adulthood, we may suddenly find that the spiritual comfort in the Psalms has stopped. We may become puzzled. Did I do something wrong? Herein lies the sweet and deep mystery of the Psalms. At this stage praying the Psalms has changed from *spiritual milk* into *solid food*, given to the spiritually mature. The Holy Spirit now opens a new depth in the treasures of the Psalms to us. Psalm-prayer feels as if it has become heavy, requiring forced concentration. It feels as if we are not being strengthened as before. The Fathers of the Church teach us that, despite what we sense, the Psalms continue to work in us at this new spiritual stage.

---

277. 1Peter 2:2
278. Hebrews 5:14

The Psalms frighten the spiritual enemies - an external work. The key to the many victories of David's military life is locked up in the knowledge that he prayed the Psalms throughout his life.

Psalms build up the inner soul - an inner work. When we pray the Psalms, we may experience much distraction and lack of fervour, a sense as if we are not praying at all, just wasting our time. This is because the enemy realises that the praying person is receiving solid food for the spiritually mature, and is being transformed, and he does not like it.

In this case the worshiper has two responsibilities:

† Focus conscientiously, and concentrate on the words of the Psalms, with perseverance and without frustration or feelings of failure, no matter how long this confrontation may take. Just continue steadfastly.

† Add another prayer time, in addition to the Psalms, a time of spontaneous prayer, to express your heart to God with faith and freedom.

In this stage God desires to deal with us inwardly. He desires to transform our image, to reveal to us the mysteries of His Kingdom.

A final word about prayer, and standing before God as priests:

Prayer is life, not merely a daily practice. This life requires regular and steadfast training. The purpose of prayer is to become a channel that connects the earthly priests with the throne of God; so that the life of God may flow in us, progressively transforming us into the image of His Son, and flow through us into a dry and weary landscape.

James 5:8: *You also, be patient. Establish your hearts, for the coming of the Lord is at hand.*

An Established Zion unit

Behold, how good and pleasant it is when brothers dwell in unity!
It is like the precious oil on the head,
running down on the beard, on the beard of Aaron,
running down on the collar of his robes!
It is like the dew of Hermon, which falls on the mountains of Zion!
For there the LORD has commanded the blessing, life forevermore.

Psalm 133

Anyone who has endeavoured to build their own house, or do a renovation project on your property, knows that the process is more than dust clouds and intruding noises, but especially characterised by stress and exhaustion. The date to sign off the house, to see the last tip being removed from the driveway, comes with deep joy and relief. Finally the day arrives when the kitchen smells like freshly baked apple-pie, coffee, and everybody is relaxed, having meaningful conversations. Building is exhilarating, but demanding. The completed project is an open door to the future, truly worth the sacrifice and inconvenience.

This roller-coaster of emotions is very earthly in comparison to what happens in the heart of God and in the heavenly places when His children build Him a place to dwell. Nobody is more eager than God Himself to see the completed project.[279] He longs to reign from within us – here on earth. He is deeply involved in all stages of building, the weighty task of digging the foundations, removing all the dirt. He is carefully watching over the stability and strength of the foundations, to last frozen winters, and summer rains. He cares about how the walls go up, to keep the world and darkness out, to protect loved ones and treasures within. The beauty of each detail lives in His heart. Beauty is not just essential to God. Beauty is the essence of God. The creation of the planet was not exclusively functional: food to eat, shade to hide from the sun etc.[280] but rather about beauty, an expression of His own image. Beauty invites us to rest. Beauty nourishes the weary and wounded. Beauty comforts pain and agony. Beauty inspires the future, and sparks creativity. Beauty is transcendent – it draws us to God.

---

279. Matthew 8:20
280. Genesis 2:9ᵃ

God cannot wait to move in. He longs for the roof to be secured, for doors to be hung, and for the last details to be polished. He is impatiently patient to take residence.

Once a Zion[281] unit is completed, God comes. We saw it in **Exodus chapter 40,** once Moses completely obeyed every instruction of God, God came in His full glory, in the same way as when Solomon completed the building of the temple as instructed by his father David.[282]

The only way for God's glory to dwell on earth, is in and through a Zion that is built and dedicated to the King.

Psalm 48:2,3: *Beautiful in elevation, the Joy of all the earth, Mount Zion...the City of the Great King. Within her citadels God has made Himself known as a fortress.*

A true Zion built and established in the eternal ways of God, holds His own people (Israel, and the Church) at the heart of this vision. And obviously, Zion always hosts His presence in the midst of His people, a glorious manifestation of His Kingdom on earth.

It is hard to conjure up visualisations of the grandeur of Kingdom units established and filled with the fullness of the glory of King.[283] Our poor response to such a majestic possibility can be compared to that of the disciples on the Mount of Transfiguration. The impact of even just a small glimpse of His unveiled, glorious presence overwhelmed them.[284] Our minds can't comprehend such magnificence,

---

281. *'ZION – Biblical Study and Vision for Ministry'* by Father Macarius (Dr Atef Meshreky) is a fully comprehensive overview of Zion as a dwelling place and throne for God on earth. ISBN 9798363232831 *www.shineinternational.org*

282. 2Chronicles 5:14

283. Ephesians 3:17

284. Mark 9:6

such joy. And our tongues are even poorer. May God grant us true spiritual vision to see with His eternal eyes that which lives in His heart.

This chapter is a preamble, not an exposition of the fruit of a true Zion unit established on earth, a place for the King to rule. These bullet points are only to awaken us to consider the immensity of such a reality. Unless the revelation grows and unfolds in our hearts with faith, until we long for nothing more than for His everlasting ways in our generation, further theological explanation will not move us.

Arise, shine; For your light has come!
And the glory of the Lord is risen upon you.
For behold, the darkness shall cover the earth,
and deep darkness the people;
But the Lord will arise over you,
and His glory will be seen upon you.
The Gentiles shall come to your light,
and kings to the brightness of your rising.
Also the sons of those who afflicted you
shall come bowing to you,
and all those who despised you
shall fall prostrate at the soles of your feet;
And they shall call you The City of the Lord,
Zion of the Holy One of Israel.

Isaiah 60:1-3,14

So, what are the benefits of entering into such a fierce battle to build a Zion in my marriage, my family, my nation?

The King of kings comes to stay

Zechariah 2:10: *Sing and rejoice, O daughter of Zion, for behold, I come and I will dwell in your midst, declares the LORD.*

The indwelling King is very zealous for Zion, as He reigns from within Zion.[285] God actually and truly entrusts His glory to her,[286] and watches over her to become His bride.[287] God dances over Zion, indeed, He rejoices with singing over Zion.[288] Zion reflects the beauty of the resident King, and His light shines upon her.

Psalm 50:2: *From Zion, the perfection of beauty, God has shined forth.*

The presence of the King directly implies that the Kingdom of God has drawn near.[289] If the King comes, everything shifts. He is so powerful, so bright and just, so beautiful. His true Person-Presence impacts everything and everybody in the immediate. Believers in Jesus will experience a fresh river of adoration. The sick are drawn to Him. Demons flee. Lives are deeply transformed. In the following passage we find just one account of Jesus coming to town: **Mark 2:1-2:** *When He returned to Capernaum after some days, it was reported that He was at home. And many were gathered together, so that there was no more room, not even at the door. And He was preaching the word to them.*

His presence bursts forth with life and power, leading to restoration and healing. His presence draws the crowds. And His presence changes the crowds. His presence

---

285. Psalms 48:2; 146:10
286. Zechariah 2:5; Psalm 102:9
287. Isaiah 62:1-5
288. Zephaniah 3:14-17
289. Matthew 5:35

overflows to bring correction, justice and righteousness in society.

But above all, the King Himself will actually dwell in our homes, in our families, and in our ministries. He is our Shepherd, our Healer and Redeemer. He is Lord and Master. But we can never forget that He is King Eternal. If He emptied Himself to be born in a humble cave in Bethlehem, how humbling that He would chose to reside at my address. As the centurion in **Matthew 8:8** said: *Lord, I am not worthy to have You come under my roof.*

What an honour to host the Great King in reality! What a joy!

Angelic Hosts Gather

Angels love God. With the King enthroned in Zion, angelic activity will increase. They love to minister to the King, to attend to each of His commands. Zion is filled with angelic worship and ministry, and intense light will accompany and overshadow all who abide there. Ministries will experience angelic accompaniment, a heavenly taste.

Mysteries being revealed

In the absence of a true Zion, mysteries are almost completely hidden from the people of God, long forgotten. The ruler of this world rules in darkness. Subsequently we can't even imagine what God wants to share with us, what our inheritance could be. We don't know that we can even long for His unsearchable riches.

Ephesians 3:8-9: *..to preach to the Gentiles the unsearchable riches of Christ, and to bring to light for everyone what is the plan of the mystery hidden for ages in God who created all things.*

The Church nowadays is content with random crumbs, and partial bits. This is a very sad state, as we contently function intellectually, influenced, even dominated by our souls, focussing only on the tangible and relational realities of ministry. If God's people continue to live in ignorance of divine, everlasting mysteries, of the strategies for the times and seasons we live in, then we are ignorant in surrendering our will for His purposes to be accomplished in our generation. Thus, we cannot be a blessing to our generation, and we will not be the carriers of Life our planet so desperately needs.

Ephesians 1:18: *Having the eyes of your hearts enlightened, that you may know ... what are the riches of His glorious inheritance in the saints.*

God's bright presence pierces all darkness, and mysteries and secrets will be revealed as He shares His heart with those who treasure His presence. His brilliant presence fills the atmosphere with light, light that is alive and life-giving.[290] His light exposes and casts out darkness.[291] But much more, it enlightens the hidden treasures, the secrets hidden for generations, the deep things of God.

Isaiah 45:3: *I will give you the treasures of darkness and the hoards in secret places, that you may know that it is I, the LORD, the God of Israel, who call you by your Name.*

---

290.   **1John 1:5:** *God is light, and in Him is no darkness at all.*
291.   Revelation 21:23

The night before His crucifixion, Jesus was with His disciples in Gethsemane. In His final conversation with His disciples, to complete their preparation and training, He said to them: **John 16:12:** *I still have many things to say to you, but you cannot bear them now.*

This remains so true for us. He has much to share with us: wisdom, revelation, understanding, insight, strategy, prayers, mysteries, warnings, callings, anointings etc. We are either unaware of the treasures available to us, or we lack interest in discovering the depths of His heart. Discovering these hidden treasures does not come cheaply. He shares His heart only with those whose lives are deeply prepared, those who treasure His secrets.

Matthew 13:10-11: *The disciples said to Him, 'Why do you speak to them in parables?' He answered, 'To you it has been given to know the secrets of the kingdom of heaven, but to them it has not been given.'*

Enduring and persevering in the warfare and hardship to build and complete a resting place for God in our hearts and lives, stirs up His love to be poured out into His people. Thus, the secrets of the Kingdom of heaven will be entrusted to us.

Zion is Attractive

First, as already said, an established Zion draws God near. He comes as King,[292] and He comes to reign.[293]

---

292.   Habakkuk 2:20
293.   John 12:15

Zechariah 9:9ª: *Rejoice greatly, O daughter of Zion! Shout, O daughter of Jerusalem! Behold, your King is coming to you; He is just and having salvation.*

Also, Zion draws the nations near, and they will receive revelation and salvation.

Isaiah 60:3-4: *Nations shall come to your light, and kings to the brightness of your rising. Lift up your eyes all around, and see; they all gather together, they come to you; your sons shall come from afar, and your daughters shall be carried on the hip.*

Zechariah 2:11: *Many nations shall join themselves to the LORD in that day, and shall be my people. I will dwell in your midst, and you shall know that the LORD of hosts has sent Me to you.*

Power for Salvation and Restoration

The King is the Lamb who was slain.

Revelation 7:17: *For the Lamb in the midst of the throne will be their shepherd, and He will guide them to springs of living water, and God will wipe away every tear from their eyes.*

Once Zion is established in our ministries, once the crucified Christ is resident on His throne, then the mysteries of the Cross and Resurrection will be revealed and released in an unhindered way, with power. Within such concentrated light, life, love and forgiveness, anyone who encounters it will enter into deep repentance and complete deliverance, leading to healing and restoration of the inner life.[294] His manifest Lordship will result in a movement of corporate

---

294. Joel 2:32

repentance without much persuasion and preaching. Who can resist His glory?

All who enter Zion will either be purified and sanctified by His fiery presence, or will flee. Zion leaves no options for indecisiveness, or lukewarmness. The complete transformation of believers is so different from the long, drawn out years of ups and downs in discipleship and counselling, without any assurance that the individual will not turn back again. The salvation proclaimed from Zion will burn deep within us the standard of heaven, and fill us with gratitude and the fear of God alike, to seal our salvation in a very deep and real way with the brilliance of God's fiery presence. This fruit will not be stolen or lost, but will last into eternity.

Zion is filled with joyful rejoicing. Ongoing praise resounds within her, and childlike freedom is restored to those in her.[295]

Yes, salvation will manifest inside Zion. And from this fortress salvation will be proclaimed to nations with authority, and be revealed widely with great impact.

Zion provides Divine Protection

Isaiah 14:32[b]: *The LORD has founded Zion, and in her the afflicted of His people find refuge.*

God, the Father and Eternal Shepherd, desires to provide protection for His children in times of danger. The Lord will fight for His loved ones against the cunning ways of the enemy.

---

295.   Psalm 9:14

Zion is a **City of Refuge** providing supernatural protection and salvation to the poor in spirit. God's children are not to be vulnerable in times of famine, in war, or anything else that may come our way as the End Times unfold. The world is shaking. God desires us to live on the heights, as if surrounded by an unseen fortress.

Zechariah 2:5ᵃ: *I will be to her a wall of fire all around, declares the LORD.*

Isaiah 32:18: *My people will abide in a peaceful habitation, in secure dwellings, and in quiet resting place.*

Zion is a **City of Peace** with no battles within her gates, but comfort, healing and joy.

Isaiah 35:10: *The ransomed of the LORD shall return and come to Zion with singing; everlasting joy shall be upon their heads; they shall obtain gladness and joy, and sorrow and sighing shall flee away.*

Christians will be exposed, just like anybody else, to natural disasters and catastrophes. If we obey His revealed wisdom, if we build Zions in our houses, then His followers will know supernatural protection and provision. This is not a cheap insurance policy, but a life lived circumspectly to prepare a place for His dwelling.

Psalm 91:9,10: *Because you have made the LORD your dwelling place— the Most High, who is my refuge — no evil shall be allowed to befall you, no plague come near your tent.*

If Zion is neglected, demonic forces will try to push inwards, to attack and cause fear and confusion, to destroy and rule.

Zion exposes, nullifies and terrifies the enemy

Psalm 48:4-5: *For behold, the kings assembled; they came together. As soon as they saw [Zion], they were astounded; they were in panic; they took to flight.*

Psalm 48 underlines several outcomes that come about once Zion is completed. When Zion is established, demons will flee, terrified and paralysed by the splendour and authority of His throne. According to verse 4 Zion causes terror to the enemy, so that they withdraw without any fierce battle. The brightness of His presence blind demons. The presence of His power overwhelms them, and scares them so they do not come near, nor influence those who dwell within the fortress. His chosen ones are safe from confusing thoughts and weakened emotions. In Zion we can hide, safe and secure, surrounded by light and truth, able to move forward in the expansion of His Kingdom, with bridal love and with much courage and boldness.[296]

So often, ministers and missionaries are spent due to the constant battles they fight. Much of our daily energy is drained and stolen from us, and not focussed or released in the actual vision received from God. We battle sickness, conflict, doubt, exhaustion - time wasted in vain. Within a true Zion, the schemes of the enemy would dissolve without endless warfare. Our days would be redeemed, and our days will be fruitful.[297]

Two cities are mentioned in **Psalm 48**. The one is Zion. The other city is mentioned in verse 7: *By the east wind you shattered the ships of Tarshish.* Tarshish is an actual demonic power that redirects the chosen of the Lord away from their

---

296.   Joshua 10:12-14
297.   Ephesians 5:15-16

calling, away from the path of obedience, driving them far away from the presence of God, as happened with Jonah.

Jonah 1:3: *Jonah arose to flee to Tarshish from the presence of the Lord. He went down to Joppa, and found a ship going to Tarshish; so he paid the fare, and went down into it, to go with them to Tarshish from the presence of the Lord.*

The power of Tarshish entices people to avoid, postpone, excuse, or not surrendering to the will of God. Instead of reaching the place that God has appointed, Nineveh in the east, Jonah sailed west to Tarshish. Tarshish directly opposes divine callings in individuals' lives, misguiding the children of God, and therefore communities struggle to fulfil their calling.

Zion has authority over the powerful ships of Tarshish that want to take us off course in life. If God is resident in our midst, these evil schemes will be exposed, and destroyed. Zion preserves the calling of God in our lives. Our youth will not waste energy trying this, and exploring that, in endless, empty circles trying to figure out their place in society. In Zion, the young and old will know their unique callings, and will be enabled to walk in it without doubt, distraction and confusing temptation to depart from God's ways. Too often we wonder whether God wants us in this place or not, although earlier we knew with certainty that God called us to be right here. But somehow we discover uncertainty in our hearts, and we start to question again if God truly called us, or not. Behind this uncertainty is actually an evil power called 'the ships of Tarshish.'

If we dwell in Zion, our divine calling is revealed and secured, and His Kingdom will advance on earth.

Nations are subdued -
our Inheritance is Restored

Psalm 2:6,8: *I have set My king on My holy hill of Zion. Ask of Me, and I will give You the nations for Your inheritance, and the ends of the earth for Your possession.*

The inheritance of nations is given to the King who is anointed in Zion, no other place. Without a Zion, our inheritance in the nations remains in the hands of ruler of this earth.

A completed Zion can and will transform nations. David built the first actual Zion, and was victorious in all his battles against the enemies of God. He subdued the heathen nations, and extended the borders of Israel beyond any other king before or after him. The neighbouring kingdoms settled peace agreements with him, and boundaries were secured for a season of peace in Israel, enjoyed by his descendant, king Solomon who did not have to fight so many wars as his father did.

Many individuals have very blessed and fruitful ministries, but without a true Zion, nations will not be transformed. When nations are subdued, it brings about a harvest of souls, and restores the honour in the nations. Zion enables nations to walk in His ways, His laws and His righteous commandments,[298] the desire and dream of any missionary. We regularly focus on too many projects, working long hours, whilst missing the bottom-line of it all. Our vision should always be to host the King, and all things will be added to us.

---

298.   Isaiah 60:1 3

Matthew 6:33: *But seek first the Kingdom of God and His righteousness, and all these things will be added to you.*

The release of the Lord's arm

Isaiah 52:10: *The LORD has bared His holy arm before the eyes of all the nations, and all the ends of the earth shall see the salvation of our God.*

Once a throne for God is established, unspeakable, supernatural miracles will follow. There will be no need, no shortfall, no sickness. There will be no danger from within (pestilence, or decay), nor will external enemies catch us off guard. There will be joy, peace, gratitude, revelation, growth, unity and authority. We will live in the extravagant abundance of heaven on earth, a new Garden of Eden.

†

Let us turn from our self-imposed business, from our personal efforts in ministry and Missions! Let us turn from individualism! May we cry out for His mercy, and entreat Him for His favour and enduring strength so that Zion may be built in us, and in our midst. Our spirits are in great need to receive this vision, the agony of God's heart, and to realise our deep need for Zions in all nations. Without Zion, the glory of the Lord cannot rest on us, and cannot shine on earth. This will hinder His purposes for His Kingdom to come with power.

The Glory of His Kingdom

It has always been in God's heart for His glory to cover the earth, for the nations to know Him and worship Him as King. We find different references to this economy of God:

Isaiah 11:9ᵇ: *For the earth shall be full of the knowledge of the LORD as the waters cover the sea.*

Habakkuk 2:14: *For the earth will be filled with the knowledge of the glory of the LORD as the waters cover the sea.*

These two scriptures are significantly different. The prophet Isaiah says that the earth will be filled with the knowledge of God, whilst Habakkuk states that the earth is to be covered with the knowledge of the glory of the Lord. The Church possesses much knowledge, but we lack the experience of glory.

Man was created for glory,[299] but lost it in the fall and was found to be naked, covered in shame. In **Romans 3:23** Apostle Paul writes: *All have sinned and fallen short of the glory of God.*

Our Saviour restored all that was lost to mankind, and in **John 17:22** He prays: *The glory that You have given Me I have given to them, that they may be one even as We are one.*

The restoration of the full manifestation of His glory within the followers of Jesus Christ, is conditional for the revelation of His Kingdom in the nations. The knowledge of His glory is not sufficient to subdue the enemy, and restore the nations. Only His actual glory will subdue all and everything to bring life, hope and a burning righteousness.

The enemy is absolutely terrified of the manifestation of the glory of God, and will go to great lengths to prevent it. He covers the nations in filth and corruption which makes it impossible for us to even consider being kings to reign with Christ. Demonic strategy discourages and depresses, creates failures and addicts, slaves without strength or vision.

---

299.   Psalm 8:4-5

As said before, even a glimpse of His glory produces fruit. The Indwelling Glory of God in Zion units takes the nations back from the enemy who has looted and stolen it, re-possesses and heals the land, restores the nations to the true King.

The absence of Zion hinders any calling from reaching its prophetic fullness.

Nations will fear the Name of the LORD,
and all the kings of the earth will fear Your glory.
For the LORD builds up Zion;
He appears in His glory;

Psalm 102:15-16

Zion in the End Times

For Zion's sake I will not hold My peace,
And for Jerusalem's sake I will not rest,
Until her righteousness goes forth as brightness,
And her salvation as a lamp that burns.
I have set watchmen on your walls, O Jerusalem;
They shall never hold their peace day or night.
You who make mention of the Lord, do not keep silent,
Give Him no rest till He establishes,
till He makes Jerusalem a praise in the earth.
And they shall call them The Holy People, The Redeemed of the Lord;
And you shall be called Sought Out, A City Not Forsaken.

Isaiah 62:1,6,7,12

Establishing Zion units is one of the essential tasks in preparing for the End Times. The full glory of God cannot dwell in our midst, or wash over the nations, until Zion is completed.

Psalm 102:16: *For the LORD builds up Zion; He appears in His glory.*

Zion provides layers of blessings for our families and ministries, but the heart of this divine strategy is to be a herald, to trumpet Christ to the nations, to proclaim His sovereign rule in the nations.

In **Exodus 19:5-6** God ordained Israel to be a 'Kingdom of Priests' – to mediate between God and the nations, and to be a 'Holy Nation' - to dwell in the midst of the nations and attract them to God's Presence. His presence in the midst of Israel made Gentile nations question their unique distinction,[300] even led them to worship the true God who is alive and personal.

In the New Testament God choses to dwell in believers, His saints who have been sanctified in reality through the grace given to us in the Messiah. God desires to dwell in the midst of His people, no longer in tents and on stones, which were only symbols of what was to come. Members of the Church are being knitted together in one Spirit to become the 'household of God,'[301] an earthly family united with angels and those already deposed in the Lord. With Jesus as the chief cornerstone, we grow into a Holy Temple for His presence. Zion is a mystical building, built with living stones, even precious stones, in becoming the new Jerusalem. God can only dwell in our midst as we live in

---

300. Psalm 147
301. Ephesians 2:19 22

true unity with His Spirit, and with one another, and His love fills our hearts.[302] If His Biblical standards are honoured and obeyed, then the cloud of glory will truly rest upon families of believers.[303]

1Peter 4:14ᵇ: *Because the Spirit of glory and of God rests upon you.*

At the Second Coming of Christ, in the final scene of the manifestation of His Kingdom on earth, this heavenly Jerusalem which has been built both on earth and in heaven, will come down from heaven, prepared as a bride for her Bridegroom,[304] and she will shine bright with the fullness of His glory.[305]

†

There should be no doubt in our hearts that God desires, and even demands of us that we build dwelling places for Him on earth. This is His divine economy to expand and establish His Kingdom to all nations.

Psalm 132:13: *For the LORD has chosen Zion; He has desired it for His dwelling place.*

In response to such a direct request, we should ask ourselves: How can my life become a Zion, a resting place for the King? What should change in my life for His rulership to be proclaimed from within my household, into nations?

---

302. Romans 5:5
303. 2Corinthians 3:18
304. Revelation 21:2-3
305. Isaiah 30:26

✝ A true Zion unit is a gathering of distinct believers who are truly transformed into Christ-likeness. She becomes the actual bride of Christ; and Christ is present in her midst as a **Bridegroom**.[306] In any encounter with a Zion unit, we will experience a divine attraction to the Bridegroom, which is impossible to ignore, or to resist.

✝ Christ is truly **King** in all members of Zion, who submit fully in all things to their Lord and Master.[307] It is not possible to host the King, whilst other lords have a place in my affairs. Once Jesus is really and truly enthroned over all the members in a particular Zion unit, His Kingdom will expand into nations.

✝ Zion has the magnetism, the ability to draw people from all walks of life to salvation. Jesus is always deeply concerned for the salvation of the **Lost**.[308] This same burden burns in the hearts of all members of Zion.

✝ As followers of Jesus, those who eagerly long for His return to earth, should prepare the **Earth,** our planet, for His public reign. We can only do this in building and establishing headquarters for His throne in our houses, and in all nations. His dwelling presence alone can sanctify and heal our planet

In the End Times the message of salvation will not reach the lost one by one, but groups and nations will be drawn to salvation as His full glory is revealed. Because Christ dwells in Zion, the heavens will be opened,[309] and the grace of salvation will be poured forth, leading to corporate conviction of souls, of families, cities, even nations.

---

306. Song of Solomon 5:10-16
307. Isaiah 26:13
308. John 3:17; John 12:47
309. Zechariah 10:1

Manifold Dimensions and Mysteries of the Gospel of Salvation have not yet been discovered. The Salvation which Christ has prepared for us is exceedingly great, continually transforming many from glory to glory. True Zion units will proclaim the full richness of the Greatness of Salvation, man being actually glorified, truly abiding and united with the Triune God, which the Early Church called *Deification.*[310] Completed salvation transforms sinners into glory.[311] Ongoing revelation will endlessly continue to renew its members, and will overflow to nations, and the land.[312] Even heaven and the heavenly hosts longs to listen to the voice of God coming from Zion, revealing endless mysteries of His Kingdom.[313]

Ephesians 3:8-10: *To me…this grace was given, to preach to the Gentiles the Unsearchable Riches of Christ, and to bring to light for everyone what is the plan of the mystery hidden for ages in God who created all things, so that through the Church the Manifold Wisdom of God might now be made known to the rulers and authorities in the heavenly places.*

The Great Commission in **Matthew 28:18-20** cannot be accomplished without His divine strategy manifesting on earth. Time is short, the labourers are few, and the harvest is great. The King within these mystical Kingdom units will subdue the earth, and nations will be shaken and drawn to salvation. The Creator and Eternal Redeemer is absolutely responsible to restore everything that was lost, including our groaning planet.

Revelation 21:5: *He who was seated on the throne said, 'Behold, I am making all things new.'*

---

310. Romans 8:17,29-30; John 17:22
311. 2Corinthians 3:18; 2Thessalonians 2:13-14; Romans 8:18
312. John 16:12,13
313. 1Peter 1:12

As Zion units are being built on earth through faithful prayer and surrendered lives, and is connected through the Spirit in a *World Salvation Net* (chapter 11), it will prepare the whole world for the glorious, public coming of the King to rule on earth.

In understanding God's economy for Salvation in the End Times, our need for this prophetic vision of Zion units, international headquarters for the King, should be proclaimed with holy zeal. Building these Zion units within our marriages and families, within our ministries and nations, should be our first and foremost priority, and should be according to His divine plans and conditions. Just as with Moses and Solomon, His instructions are exact and detailed. In our longing for His glory, we should only build according to His eternal Word.

Matthew 7:24: *Everyone then who hears these words of Mine and does them will be like a wise man who built his house on the rock.*

*Let this be recorded for a generation to come,
so that a people yet to be created may praise the LORD:
that He looked down from His holy height;
from heaven the LORD looked at the earth,
to hear the groans of the prisoners,
to set free those who were doomed to die,
that they may declare in Zion the Name of the LORD,
and in Jerusalem His praise,
when peoples gather together, and kingdoms,
to worship the LORD.*

Psalm 102:18-22

Epilogue

The Throne of God

Blessed are poor in spirit, for yours is the kingdom of God.

Luke 6:20

The Holy Spirit grants revelation to us according to our measure of faith and calling. There is no instant download. We grow step by step, little by little, as true revelation takes time to mature until it is fully revealed and established in our lives. As the Holy Spirit opens up this particular revelation of His authority in our hearts, it becomes a source of energy within us to focus day by day, to see His Kingdom on earth as it is in heaven.

Nothing is more humbling as a meditation on His Throne, to stir a longing in us for His Kingdom to manifest in our generation. This chapter is an after-thought, the cherry on this cake! You are welcome!

†

The Throne is the chair of God, the chair of Christ, as King. It is not a physical chair in a particular palace, but a spiritual chair reaching beyond time.

Psalm 11:4ª: *The LORD is in His holy temple; the LORD's Throne is in heaven.*

His Kingdom is over all nations, not primarily over the angelic hosts in the heavenlies.

Psalm 103:19: *The LORD has established His Throne in the heavens, and His Kingdom rules over all nations.*

There is no end to His throne. His throne will last forever and ever.

Psalm 45:6: *Your Throne, O God, is forever and ever. The sceptre of Your Kingdom is a sceptre of righteousness.*

This knowledge can either be a false comfort to us, giving us licence to rest and wait to see how things will pan out. Or, this knowledge can energise us to get involved in revealing His everlasting kingdom, to see the fullness of its extension and manifestation on earth, even in my life-time.

If this was all we knew about His throne, we might feel a bit left out, as if outside the picture. These passages seem so distant, very spiritual and nearly irrelevant to our lives. Although God has a spiritual throne in heaven, it is real. Human beings have been able to see this heavenly throne.

Isaiah 6:1: *In the year that King Uzziah died I saw the Lord sitting upon a Throne, high and lifted up; and the train of His robe filled the temple.*

The New Testament sheds light on the place of His throne.

Revelation 4:2,4,8-11: *At once I was in the Spirit, and behold, a Throne stood in heaven, with One seated on the throne. Around the Throne were twenty-four thrones, and seated on the thrones were twenty-four elders, clothed in white garments, with golden crowns on their heads. The four living creatures, each of them with six wings, are full of eyes all around and within, and day and night they never cease to say, 'Holy, holy, holy, is the Lord God Almighty, who was and is and is to come!' And whenever the living creatures give glory and honour and thanks to Him who is seated on the Throne, who lives forever and ever, the twenty-four elders fall down before Him who is seated on the Throne and worship Him who lives forever and ever. They cast their crowns before the Throne, saying, 'Worthy are You, our Lord and God, to receive glory and honour and power, for You created all things, and by Your will they existed and were created.'*

God's throne is clearly the absolute centre of all worship. This alone is enough motivation to discover the place of His Throne on earth, so that we can worship Him who is enthroned throughout the ages, forever and ever.

Matthew 25:31: *When the Son of Man comes in His glory, and all the angels with Him, then He will sit on His glorious Throne.*

In this verse the throne is ascribed to the Son of Man, the incarnated God-man. In other words, the human Jesus is seated on a glorious throne. But where is this throne? Christ, the incarnated human being will have a throne on earth in His second coming. And yet, the throne of God is always synonymous with the Trinity, who is eternally enthroned in heaven.

Our responsibility

Thrones demand obedience from its subjects. In the heavenly scene there is much worship and complete submission to the Throne of God. Is our primary responsibility on earth to simply direct all of our worship to heaven, to obey and submit to Him? If this is true, then we are left in a passive stance before His throne.

Is there nothing else His earthy followers should do?

Indeed, God has a much higher calling on His people, to actively participate in His Kingdom, both on earth and in heaven. May this mystery really open up in our hearts.

God's throne, His rulership is in heaven. The earth was given to Adam. As Adam was created in God's image, He represented the Eternal King on earth, and was granted an actual throne to rule. There was a condition to Adam's throne: his authority was to be submitted to God in heaven, as Adam's earthly throne was only an extension of God's heaven throne.

If Adam had never fallen, his descendants would all have had thrones, each in a dedicated place on earth. These thrones would not have opposed each other, but rather served the glorious King in true unity and sweet harmony. The character of these thrones would have been different from what we experience today about earthly thrones. If we consider that the Constitution of the Kingdom of God is declared in the Beatitudes,[314] then these earthly thrones would have been meek, humble, righteous, merciful, pure in heart, making peace etc. It is unimaginable to contemplate the extent to which the Kingdom of God would have brought life on Earth.

Satan stole this earthly throne from Adam, and the earth was enslaved to Satan in the fall.

1John 5:19: *We know that we are from God, and the whole world lies in the power of the evil one.*

Romans 8:20: *For all creation was subjected to futility, not willingly, but because of him who subjected it.*

Restoring the Throne of God to Mankind

How did Jesus, our Redeemer, restore the throne of Adam? This is such a subtle revelation, so easy to miss in our big and important ministries.

The essence of God's throne is servanthood. Adam was created to serve the earth! Adam was commissioned in **Genesis 2:15:** *The LORD God took the man and put him in the garden of Eden to work it and keep it.*

---

314.   Matthew 5:1-12

He was created in the image of a Servant King, to 'work' and 'keep' the earth, not to lord it over the earth.

Satan, on the other hand, is superior, and all his deeds are profoundly self-centred. His bait in deceiving Eve was to tease her pride, her ego.

Genesis 3:5: *For God knows that in the day you eat of [this fruit] your eyes will be opened, and you will be like God, knowing good and evil.*

From the moment the idea that 'you will be like God' entered into her heart, she became greedy for gain. She wanted to be more than who she was created. The poison of pride entered human nature: the corruption of selfishness, self-importance, and wanting to be a god, or like God, wanting to be higher than others. She lost her servant heart. Ever since, we continued to wrestle over position and titles, wanting to be first, the best, to be acknowledged. We don't like submission. We detest humiliation. We don't want to be left out. We don't want to serve. Life has got to go my way. We believe that we know better than others, so it would be good for them to listen to us!

In the fall, everything that God intended for man and creation, was turned up-side down. The Devil came to possess the throne on earth, and subsequently kings and rulers became authoritative and greedy, dominating dictators, and powerful oppressors, even abusers. Satan's rule is characterised by egoistic individualism, self-interest, rebellion, leading to destruction. As a result we sit with layers of societal classes; the powerful and the nobodies, the famous and the faceless, the have's and the have-not's. The entitled, and the migrant. There is little peace or respect between these classes, rather a brewing animosity, jealousy, and often hatred of each other.

But God never changes. His Kingdom can only extend through the descendants of Adam. He is undeterred by the fall. God always does the same things: 6000 years ago, in 2022, and especially in the End Times: God wants to entrust mankind with His throne on earth. Therefore, after the Fall, God did not remove free-will from mankind, although we see the imprint of Satan's authority on all kings, politicians, parents and any person in a position of leadership, as we automatically inherit the notion of being selfish, the misuse of privilege and authority. Fallen nature is ruling a fallen world.

God, being faithful, offers each king in each generation the chance of servanthood and righteousness. The Holy Spirit knocks on the heart of each leader in a different way. Will they respond to the humble call of the Holy Spirit? Will they serve their subjects in justice and humility? Will they care for the poor, the orphaned, being a shepherd for the crowds? Some respond positively. Many don't.

Biblical examples throughout History

· Pharaoh

Pharaoh, the mighty king of Egypt, met Joseph when he interpreted his dreams.

Genesis 41:38,40: *Pharaoh said to his servants, 'Can we find a man like this, in whom is the Spirit of God? You shall be over my house, and all my people shall order themselves as you command. Only in regard the throne will I be greater than you.'*

Despite the social distance between Pharaoh and Joseph, Pharaoh recognised the greatness in this ragged prisoner. Pharaoh made Joseph ruler over his household, even his nation. Pharaoh heard the wisdom of the Holy Spirit in Joseph, and he submitted to it. True authority requires obedience, and obedience requires humility - to bow before wisdom! Pharaoh's trust in, and submission to Joseph, a worshipper of the God of Israel, brought life to many. The consequence of Pharaoh's humility was that God saved many nations from famine, including the Jews.

A few years later Joseph brought his father, Jacob to Egypt.

Genesis 47:7: *Joseph brought in Jacob his father and stood him before Pharaoh, and Jacob blessed Pharaoh.*

Did you miss it? Who blessed who? Who is the greatest? The one who blesses is considered greater than the one receiving the blessing. To receive a blessing, we bow before the greater who would put his hands upon us. Pharaoh was always considered to be a god on earth in his own right. And yet we find that Pharaoh acknowledges that Jacob is greater than him, and he longingly bows his head before Jacob.

This bowing of the god of Egypt acknowledged the Throne of God in Jacob to be greater than his own earthly kingdom. In this mysterious way, the Kingdom of God manifested on earth through the righteous, God-fearing life of Jacob, and many nations were saved from death. The Throne of God within Egypt pushed back the kingdom of Death.

Satan despised this act of humility, and came up with new ways to regain rulership in Egypt. The Jews multiplied, and became a powerful nation over ~400 years. They worshipped YHWH, the God who is Adonai, literally meaning Lord. In other words, there was a throne in the midst of Egypt where the heavenly King ruled on earth. Satan wants to establish his own throne on earth in each generation. So, he brought about a new Pharaoh to the throne.

Exodus 1:8-10: *Now there arose a new king over Egypt, who did not know Joseph. He said to his people, 'Behold, the people of Israel are too many and too mighty for us. Let us deal shrewdly with them.'*

Satan always rules through injustice and oppression. He intended to kill all the Jewish boys, desiring to destroy their hope for a Messiah. But God raised up Moses to bring Israel out of Egypt. We are familiar with the clash between the two kingdoms, the kingdom of the God of Israel, and the kingdom of the Egyptian gods, which led to their utter humiliation in the ten plagues.[315] Finally, the Red Sea opened up to bring the people of God to safety, while Pharaoh and all his chariots, including his ego, drowned.

A new Beginning

In the wilderness God started to teach His people about His Kingdom, how not to be slaves, but a royal priesthood. How does healthy authority function in society? How does His throne function on earth?

Authority works through structure. Therefore, God organised all twelve tribes; there were those over thousands, those over hundreds, fifties, and over tens.[316] This is an everlasting, divine approach, to have a shepherd for the flock, a father for the family, a head for the body, a bishop for the Church. God established structure in society with elders as leaders, and within families for husbands to be the head.

Whenever there is no structure, Satan will always somehow become the head.

---

315.   Exodus 7-12
316.   Exodus 18:25

Within this divine organisation and administration His divine throne functions on earth. Each tribe had a leader, the head of the house of his fathers,[317] with meetings ordained for specific leaders.[318] These leaders could not function in their own strength and preferences.

Numbers 11:16: *The LORD said to Moses, 'Gather for Me seventy men of the elders of Israel, whom you know to be the elders of the people and officers over them, and bring them to the tent of meeting, and let them take their stand there with you.'*

God took from the spirit of Moses and put it on the seventy elders, and they 'ruled' over Israel in one spirit. There was no competition, comparison, or individual expression of personal preference. One ego could not supersede the other. All acknowledged and submitted to the Presence of the great King in their midst.

God nurtured a culture of obedience. If we obey His commandments, if we submit to His Lordship, His wisdom, His laws and rules, His timing, then He protects and blesses.[319] This brings peace and prosperity to all in the camp. We know what happened to the few who did things their own way, for example Korah,[320] and Achan in the battle of Ai.[321] Their disobedience to the structures that God instituted effected all Israel, and very definitely their immediate families.

Society, and especially the church, has become weary of organisational structures – with good reasons. Due to twisted headship, corruption, even oppression, we

---

317. Number 1:4
318. Numbers 10:4
319. Deuteronomy 28
320. Numbers 26:8-10
321. Joshua 7

find ourselves quite sceptical to authoritative structures. We don't trust their underlying intentions. We want to demolish suffocating hierarchies, and rebuild in our own 'organic' and democratic ways where each person has equal say and weight. We promote individuality and encourage free thinking. We have simply grown to detest authority.

Joshua

After Moses, Joshua shepherded God's people.

Numbers 27:15-18: *Moses spoke to the LORD, 'Let the LORD, the God of the spirits of all flesh, appoint a man over the congregation who shall go out before them and come in before them, who shall lead them out and bring them in, that the congregation of the LORD may not be as sheep that have no Shepherd.' So the LORD said to Moses, 'Take Joshua the son of Nun, a man in whom is the Spirit, and lay your hand on him.'*

Shepherds serve. A shepherd lays down his life for his sheep. Both Joshua and David were anointed to be shepherds over God's people.

2Samuel 5:2^b: *The LORD said, 'You shall be Shepherd of My people Israel, and you shall be prince over Israel.'*

These mighty military men, these heroes in all history, were not anointed to be kings to lord it over inferior subjects. Both Joshua and David are presenting us with a mirror image of Jesus, the Shepherd King, serving those entrusted to them.

Matthew 9:36: *When [Jesus] saw the crowds, He had compassion on them, because they were harassed and helpless, like sheep without a Shepherd.*

At the end of the Peter's life, in giving his final instructions to those who would lead the church, he wrote in **1Peter 5:2-3:** *Shepherd the flock of God that is among you, exercising oversight, not under compulsion, but willingly, as God would have you; not for shameful gain, but eagerly; not domineering over those in your charge, but being examples to the flock.*

True leadership manifests in authority as a shepherd. True leadership can never function with dismissive indifference. Under the leadership of a shepherd, all in society prospers, from the youngest and the least, to the mighty and the rich.

This remains a struggle in all generations. Consider the kingship of Saul, Solomon, Ahab, the Romans, the Greek empire, the British empire, the World Wars, Communism, Apartheid, Islam, Capitalism etc. Throughout the ages we always find perverted authority lording it over others.

Any leader who has not acquired the Spirit of Christ, is vulnerable to be a selfish lord. The fruit of this demonic leadership in the nations is ongoing agony for humanity, and the planet.

Israel demanded a king

During the period of the Judges God's people rejected authority and structure.[322] Everybody did what he thought right in his own eyes – a slippery slope. This lead to perversion and anarchy. Israel was far removed from the authority of the throne of God, and they demanded a king, just like other nations.[323]

---

322. Judges 21:25
323. 1Samuel 8:5b

Saul became king.[324] He was tall and handsome. He ruled in his own ways. He did not submit to the authority of the prophet Samuel. He did not obey God's commands. His throne brought no life on earth, and no glory to God among the nations.

In His covenant love for Israel, God graciously appointed a ruddy shepherd boy as the next king. **David's** heart was connected with, and submitted to the ways and purposes of the heavenly Throne.

Acts 13:22: *I have found in David the son of Jesse a man after My heart, who will do all My will.*

David understood that there is a seen and an unseen throne, a heavenly and an earthly throne. David represented God's throne on earth. His kingdom was not his own.

At the end of David's reign, we find two passages that describe his rulership:
1Kings 2:12: *Solomon sat on the throne of David his father, and his kingdom was firmly established.*

The throne was called after David, and it was a good throne. Solomon inherited this throne from his father, a throne with authority and favour among nations.

In **1Chronicles 29:23** we find a different description of this throne: *Then Solomon sat on the throne of the LORD as king in place of David his father.*

Here David's throne is called the Throne of God! God ruled through David on earth, an extension of God's heavenly authority.

---

324.   1Samuel 10

This is the first time this term, 'God's throne on earth', is used in scripture. How significant!

Empires

In response to David's success and rulership among the nations, Satan came up with new strategies to hinder the Throne of God on earth. He raised up powerful empires, all opposing the nation of Israel. Why would mighty nations like Egypt, Babylon and Rome be so concerned about a little nation in the desert?

Because Satan wants to rule on the Throne of God on earth!

Nebuchadnezzar was a great king, symbolised by the head of gold in the dream given from God, considered to be a god himself. When Daniel, only a civil servant and exile, interpreted his dreams, something happened in the heart of this great king.

Daniel 2:46-47: *King Nebuchadnezzar fell on his face and paid homage to Daniel, and commanded that an offering and incense be offered up to him. The king said to Daniel, 'Truly, your God is God of gods, and Lord of kings, a revealer of mysteries, for you have been able to reveal this mystery.'*

In actuality, the Babylonian empire fell down before the God of Israel. Nebuchadnezzar even burnt incense to Daniel. The throne of the Great I Am was once again mystically established on earth. Satan's plans backfired.

The Messianic Throne

The only begotten Son of God is the King. He is the new Adam, to 'work and keep' the earth.[325] He extended heavenly rulership for the prosperity of all on earth. Jesus became the true Shepherd for the lost sheep of Israel, caring for those oppressed by demons and sickness, laying down His life for the sheep.[326]

Jesus is a humble King, and His Kingdom serves all, even sinners. The Septuagint translation of **Psalm 96:10** reads as follows:
Say among the nations that the LORD reigns on wood! Yes, the world is established; it shall never be moved; He will judge the peoples with equity.

Modern translations only read: *Say among the nations that the Lord reigns*, but the Septuagint[327] (Ps 95:10) proclaims that *the Lord reigns on wood*.

The Jews, after the Resurrection of Jesus, blotted these words out from future translations, because of the astounding evidence it proclaimed that Jesus was the Messiah, who died on wood. Thank God that this translation was preserved through the ages, as it carries such a key to understanding His Kingdom on earth.

Psalm 96:10ª: *Say among the nations that the LORD reigns on wood!*

---

325. Genesis 2:15
326. John 10:11-14
327. The **Septuagint** is the Greek translation of the Jewish Old Testament, translated 300-250BC by seventy Jewish scribes. Greek scriptures were widely used in the time of Jesus, and during early Christianity, as non-Jewish nations could not read Hebrew. The text of the Septuagint is quoted more often than the original Hebrew text in the Greek New Testament (particularly in Paul's epistles), and also by the later Apostolic Church Fathers.

The incarnated Jesus' throne is made of wood, referring to the salvation Jesus brought about in surrendering His life on the cross. Jesus turned authority upside down. He started His life as a baby King, emptied, humble and poor.[328] He was born in a stall, became a refugee, was distrusted and overlooked all His life. He was accused, misunderstood, misjudged, and constantly questioned.[329] He was never offended. And He never defended Himself. He healed many, especially the demon possessed. He exposed the false authority of the Pharisees and scribes, whilst having no place Himself to lay His own head. He was an equal of the crowds who needed Him – just a carpenter walking the hills of Galilea.

Jesus did only what He saw His Father was doing.[330] He never walked in independence. He never came up with any bright ideas. He submitted and obeyed like a servant. Indeed, blessed are the poor in spirit, for theirs is the Kingdom of Heaven.

In the fullness of time, He confronted the kingdom of Satan by dying on a wooden cross.

John 19:19: *Pilate wrote an inscription and put it on the cross. It read, 'Jesus of Nazareth, the King of the Jews.'*

There, Jesus hung on the cross, enthroned on wood, outside Jerusalem, for all to see. King of the Jews! He is serving and shepherding all nations and all generations, whilst completely destroying the throne of the ruler of this world. His rulership is one of forgiveness and love,[331] of meekness and obedience.[332]

---

328.   Philippians 2:7
329.   Psalm 56:5; Matthew 22:15; Luke 11:53,54; 15:1-2; 20:20; Mark 3:22; John 11:53
330.   John 5:19
331.   Luke 23:34
332.   Luke 22:42

Jesus restored God's throne on earth through obedience and suffering, even unto death.[333]

Golgotha was a raw power encounter between two kingdoms, the Kingdom of Life and Light, and the Kingdom of Death. He entered Death and broke its power over all mankind.

In the Second Coming of Jesus we will see the full manifestation of His Throne on earth:

Matthew 19:28: *Truly, I say to you, in the new world, when the Son of Man will sit on His glorious Throne, you who have followed Me will also sit on twelve thrones, judging the twelve tribes of Israel.*

Jesus will again rule on earth, and the apostles will also have thrones with Him. The apostles will represent Adam, all mankind, on thrones, on earth. Jesus will rule, together with mankind, on earth, as was His intention since before creation. But on that day He will not rule on wood, but in glory!

Mankind will not rule in heaven, but on earth. And yet, the throne of man will be united with the Throne of Jesus. This is completed redemption: the throne of Adam restored on earth, a throne that serves the eternal Throne in Heaven. One Kingdom. One King.

†

A sad phenomenon in our generation is that the church no longer carries our cross daily. There may be a cross on the steeple, or on the Church logo, but no longer is the

---

333.   Hebrews 5:8; Philippians 2:8

cross engraved in our hearts, in our days, seared into our lives. We don't 'rule on wood'. We avoid pain at all cost, especially humiliation and injustice. Every one of us wants to be unique, and outstanding, striving to build our own platform, to make our voice heard. We fight for ourselves, promote ourselves, and are constantly offended. We want an increase in anointing, whilst resisting accountability and hardship. We want to raise big finances for strategic projects, whilst our eyes are dry, not weeping for the suffering and lost. We even take courses in how to leave a legacy – to look great after we have died.

As Jesus was approaching the cross, His wooden throne, His disciples were disagreeing about who was the greatest, about who could sit at His right and His left hand in the Kingdom of heaven. These are Jesus' final instructions to them as He was preparing them to rule:

Mark 10:42-45: *You know that those who are considered rulers of the Gentiles lord it over them, and their great ones exercise authority over them. But it shall not be so among you. But whoever would be great among you must be your servant, and whoever would be first among you must be slave of all. For even the Son of Man came not to be served but to serve, and to give His life as a ransom for many.*

God longs for people, men and women, who will live in obedience and submission to His commandments, who will live in the power of the cross as true shepherds, lives deeply characterised by the wooden cross. These will be accompanied by authorative angels, and their prayers and lives will break the power of the throne of Satan on earth. They will impact nations, not just congregations. The Throne of God will be manifest through them on earth.

May God show us favour and bless us;
may He truly show us his favour.
Selah.
Let your ways be known by all the nations of the earth,
along with Your deliverance.
Let the people thank You, God.
Let all the people thank You.
Let the nations rejoice and sing for joy,
because You judge people with fairness
and You govern the people of the earth.
Selah.
Let the people thank You, God;
let all the people thank You.
May the earth yield its produce.
May God, our God, bless us.
May God truly bless us
so that all the peoples of the earth will fear Him.

Psalm 67

References

(2023) *Zion – A Scriptural Study and A Vision of Ministry.* Arizona: Shine International.

Atef Meshreky. (2015) *Kingdom of God & The End Times.* Seoul, Korea: Anchor Publishing & Media.

Atef Meshreky. (2016) *The Inner man & The Formation of Christ.* Arizona: Shine International.

All these are available on Amazon.com, and Shineinternational.org

About the Author

Ina Steyn grew up in Namibia on an African sheep farm, and experienced a calling to serve the Lord in the nations at a young age. She was privileged to be exposed to multiple expressions of modern-day Missions in many nations. She started in administrative work in Southern Africa, and partook in Church-planting in Siberia in the early 90's. The disappointment of unanswered prayer lead her to Scotland, where she served in Intercession ministries, and started an Internship to walk alongside young missionaries. During this season she also served in Western Europe alongside leadership teams of fourteen nations. She was privileged to travel extensively to many European nations over two decades, meeting with teams and individuals in leadership, and in personal capacities. She has been living in England since 2008.

She writes with due respect to those whom she had the honour to rub shoulders with, those who truly give their lives to serve His Kingdom in Europe. This book was not written as a critique of the different views in the arena of wrestling with our place in the Kingdom of God. Rather, may this book serve us to grasp a deeper understanding of the ancient ways, the eternal *economia* of God. May this book enable us to align the revelation and enthusiasm which God has granted us already to see His Kingdom come in our generation, with His eternal blueprint for the earth: to rule as priest-kings.